THE GOSPEL

ACCORDING TO THE

DaVINCI
CODE

THE GOSPEL
ACCORDING TO THE
DaVINCI
CODE

THE TRUTH BEHIND
THE WRITINGS OF DAN BROWN

Kenneth Boa &
John Alan Turner

BROADMAN
& HOLMAN
PUBLISHERS

NASHVILLE, TENNESSEE

13-digit ISBN: 978-0-8054-4190-1
10-digit ISBN: 0-8054-4190-5

Published by Broadman & Holman Publishers,
Nashville, Tennessee

Dewey Decimal Classification: 273
Subject Heading: BROWN, DAN—CRITICISM \ GNOSTICISM
CHRISTIAN LIFE

Bible passages are from the New International Version, copyright © 1973,
1978, 1984 by International Bible Society.

06 07 08 09 10   10 9 8 7 6 5 4 3 2 1

With gratitude to God for our wives,

Karen and Jill

CONTENTS

ACKNOWLEDGMENTS

From Ken:

More than individuals, we were meant to become communal persons, weaving our identities from the fine threads of relationships and experiences.

By the grace and loving-kindness of God, I have been richly blessed with a wealth of people who have loved, encouraged, taught, mentored, and shaped me through my sojourn thus far. Specific to this book, I thank my associate Bill Ibsen for his work with me on our *Unraveling The Da Vinci Code* DVD along with other presentations.

From John:

I used to think books were written in isolation—the pained author laboring alone to capture the exact sentiment with precise words. Now I know better. Writing, like life, is best performed in the context of community. The resulting process is not only more enjoyable, but also produces a much better product.

That being the case, I thank the community that helped me on this project, beginning with the people at The reThink Group. You gave me enough time and space to finish two books. Thanks to Reggie Joiner, Leigha Montgomery, and especially Jeff Sandstrom. Thanks to Melanie Williams and Greg Payne for not getting too upset at my missing other deadlines to make this one.

Anne-Geri Fann, you could get a job teaching people how to write introductions and conclusions. Without your help, this book would never have ended.

The Monday Night Guys' Group endured more mind-numbing speeches from me about church history, art history, literary criticism, and the Nag Hammadi documents than anyone should ever have to hear. Those Monday nights provided me with some much-needed sanity maintenance.

The Wednesday night Bible study I teach at the North Atlanta Church of Christ prayed consistently for this book and my family. Thank you.

Thanks to all the readers of my blog who contributed comments on this subject—from the sublime to the ridiculous. We all remain "in his big grip."

Phil Pierce, you are the fastest reader I've ever known. Your research gave me a lot of information early on that allowed me to think about the big ideas contained here.

Bill Winegardner, thanks for reading the chapter at the cabin and telling me it wasn't too deep. If it had been, I might have stopped and never written another word.

Sandra Morales, you always called at just the right time to make me laugh, usually resulting in something coming out of my nose.

Of course, there are all the authors I've been influenced by. I've stolen ideas from many of you. I've stolen a way of thinking from even more of you. Stephen Mansfield, John Ortberg, Norm Geisler, Ravi Zacharias, Philip Yancey, Mortimer J. Adler, C. S. Lewis, J. P. Moreland, Peter Kreeft, Paul Copan—the list could go on and on until Jesus returns.

Four more people, and we're done.

A lady named Dona Cornutt is in her eighties and lives in Pampa, Texas. If it weren't for her, I might not have given much thought to becoming a writer. Thank you, Dona. I made it.

My dad, Dr. J. J. Turner, taught me to search for truth and not be afraid of where truth takes you. He is a lifelong learner, and I am proud to be a chip off that old block.

Dr. B, you have been Jesus to my family and me. I do not know how we would have survived the past three years if not for you. I would not have been given the chance to write this if you hadn't offered. You're not only the smartest man I know, you may very well be the most Christlike as well.

And then there's my wife, Jill. You probably wrote more of this book than I did. You had the overwhelming task of taking my brain dumps and turning them into beautiful chapters. You had the even more overwhelming task of raising our daughters and living with me at the same time. You're not only my editor; you're my best friend and my partner in all things. That is very good news to me.

INTRODUCTION

Given our radical discontinuity with the past,
we must restate Christian faith in a manner that takes
full account of an anti-Christian . . . universe.
— Leonard Sweet, *Post-Modern Pilgrims*

*I*n April 2005, in an article titled "The Novel that Ate the World," *Time* magazine announced that Dan Brown was one of the 100 most influential people in the world today. The same list included Christian heavyweights Rick Warren, John Stott, and (ironically) the man who would be named pope of the Roman Catholic Church at the end of that very month, Joseph Cardinal Ratzinger.

This year's influencers, *Time*'s managing editor Jim Kelly said, had made their mark by "moral influence" rather than political power. For those of us in the Christian community, it's easy to see how much influence men like Warren, Stott, and Ratzinger have. But according to *Time*, Dan Brown has the same "moral influence" as those three men. If that's true, then the work of these three great men (and countless others who go unnamed) is being countered by a heretical former English teacher from Exeter, New Hampshire, who just happened to write an international best-seller.

Still, when we told people we were working on this book, we heard the familiar refrain of "Why? It's only fiction." Well, according to *Time*, it's not only fiction; it's "moral influence." *Time* editor Jim Kelly understands Dan Brown correctly. Brown is not merely writing fiction; he, like most writers, espouses a particular worldview. Read without discernment, his fiction creates confusion and fosters the cynical attitude that too many people already struggle with, making it harder than ever for them to hear the true gospel.

Dan Brown is not the Antichrist. Nor is he part of some conspiracy to take over the world. After spending the last several months getting to know Dan Brown through his writings and interviews (he never responded to our invitation to talk), we're not even sure he understands why Christians think his books are such a big deal.

Maybe Dan Brown isn't such a bad guy. But he is a voice, shouting loudly the war cries of an ideology set on destroying the faith of a generation characterized by "uncertainty, insecurity, and doubt," says author Judith Stacey in *Brave New Families*.[1] What Dan Brown says he believes is fundamentally incompatible with historic, orthodox Christianity. However, in a pluralistic society such as ours, millions of people seem to think you can pick and choose your beliefs like toppings on your pizza. Who is to say that pepperoni and mushrooms is better than sausage and black olives?

For these people, Christians and non-Christians alike, Dan Brown has slopped together a pile of foundationless facts and laid them atop a not-so-well-hidden agenda. Among his "Bible scholars" are a fiction writer, a holder of a master's degree in German who recently spoke at the National Crop Circles Convention, and a group of men who have claimed in other books that the Shroud of Turin was painted by Leonardo da Vinci and that the great pyramids of Egypt were likely built by extraterrestrials. The theory that is the foundation for the entire novel has been proven a fraud and been confessed (in convincing detail) by its perpetrator.

It took us a few hours to research the names on the "partial bibliography" listed on Brown's own Web site (www.danbrown.com) to uncover the nature and character of his sources. Anyone could have done it, but for some reason, most people haven't. Perhaps it's because Brown has heaped the pile of misinformation so high that people don't know where to start. Sifting through it could take more time than the average reader of cheap thrillers has to invest.

Unfortunately, this has left us much like the crowd in Hans Christian Andersen's tale, *The Emperor's New Clothes*, singing the praises of this "master craftsman's" invisible erudition. "How impeccable his research! See how his facts fit together and how compellingly he crafts a scene!" At some point in time, someone must step forward and shout, "He's naked!"

Granted, there have been some whistle-blowers in the past couple of years. Among our favorites are Darrell L. Bock's *Breaking the Da Vinci Code* (Thomas Nelson, 2004), Ben Witherington III's *The Gospel Code: Novel Claims About Jesus, Mary Magdalene and Da Vinci* (InterVarsity, 2004), and Carl E. Olson and Sandra Miesel's *The Da Vinci Hoax* (Ignatius Press, 2004). Plenty of books have been written about Dan Brown's *The Da Vinci Code*, enough that we didn't think it necessary to write another about all of the historical, artistic, and theological errors contained in it. But even after a slew of books, articles, and hours of talk radio have exposed Dan Brown's factual errors, the runaway train that is *The Da Vinci Code* and its influence continues headlong.

So, perhaps another approach is warranted. Maybe, instead of examining *what* Dan Brown got wrong in *The Da Vinci Code,* we should explore some of the reasons *why* he gets things wrong in the first place. Maybe if we can figure that out, we won't have to write a follow-up for everything else he publishes—if he ever publishes anything again. See, it is our firm belief that Dan Brown writes what he writes because he believes what he believes. Rather than dealing with effects (Dan Brown's controversial novels), we want to deal with what we think is the cause (Dan Brown's faulty worldview).

The fact that most of us are buying Brown's theories without any inquiry says something alarming about who we are. We are a culture of people too eager to doubt and not quick enough to investigate. We trust a man who relies on unexamined pseudo-scholarship and are ready to scrap an orthodox belief that's withstood 2,000 years of intense scrutiny.

In the September/October 1991 issue of *Family Therapy Networker,* researchers Maureen O'Hara and Walter Anderson had this to say about the generation we are now living as part of: "The postmodern world is shaped by pluralism, democracy, religious freedom, consumerism, mobility, and increasing access to news and entertainment. Residents of this postmodern world are able to see that there are many beliefs, multiple realities, and an exhilarating but daunting profusion of world views—a society that has lost its faith in absolute truth and in which people have to choose what to believe."[2]

We are becoming a frightened people who don't know what to believe or who to trust. And because we have lost a continuity of culture (few of us sit down with our grandparents and listen to their stories anymore), we no longer trust history. We don't find out how we got here, and we can't see the role that we play in history. In the scramble to figure out where we are when we've refused to learn about where we've been, our Jesus, who is "the same yesterday and today and forever" (Heb. 13:8), becomes just another great man—one we can mold and shape into whatever we want or need him to be.

Dan Brown has capitalized on our discontinuity by writing his own religion, and his disciples are signing on in droves.

But the gospel according to Dan Brown is no gospel at all. It is bitterly sad news. From Brown we learn that history cannot be relied upon, that the people in our lives whom we've trusted most have been lying to us to suit their own agendas. The truth that has held together for 2,000 years is a lie. The very cornerstones of Western civilization are defective. We who believe we have a personal relationship with Jesus the Messiah, born of a virgin and raised from the dead, are pitifully misled. Dan Brown says he is a Christian, but that everyone's definition of *Christian* is different, and we're all fine as long as we continue on our own paths to enlightenment—a statement that initially sounds full of depth, but probed deeper is a hollow substitute for those searching for truth.

How is it Christians stand by and let this happen? Maybe some of us dedicated one Sunday or Wednesday night Bible study to dispel the theories of this internationally influential author. But for the most part, we've attended to other matters while he's stolen away with our Christ and replaced him with a mere man.

Who is telling our story? Why aren't we gathering our forces and standing up to defend the single most powerful and wonderful idea in the history of the world? Why don't the books we write sell 40 million copies? Bruce Wilkinson and Rick Warren may have given Dan Brown a run for his money, but there ought to be hundreds of authors lined up with books filled with life-changing ideas. Our story is better! Where are the Christian authors? Where are the Christian artists, scientists, inventors, and educators? We hold fast to a truth that has the power to rock the world and make a story like Brown's a laughingstock. We believe in one so influential and so really resurrected from the dead that he can save even this bewildered generation.

If Dan Brown's book leads us to anything, it should lead us to think about the way we use our influence and the way we model the life of the one who drives history. We should accept it as a challenge to cast the light of truth and brighten the world in which we live, even if that world has become apathetic to its own darkness.

If anyone is going to restate the Christian faith, it ought to be us, the ones who believe it. We ought to be giving up battles among ourselves and dedicating our time to studying our Bibles, our history, and our culture in preparation for becoming the most well-informed, influential, and best-behaved people this world has ever seen. And may we do so on our knees before Jesus Christ, the only divine code that can break the allure of Dan Brown's non-gospel.

Chapter 1

WHY NOW?

Taking the Fork in the Road

Western society stands at a crossroads. To the right we find an adaptation of modernity: an honest appraisal of how tenuous our grasp on absolute truth is and a conscious decision to maintain our convictions with humility. To the left we have postmodernity: a total denial of absolutes and the insistence that one must discover truth for him- or herself. The path we choose will, in large part, determine the future of our society. Dan Brown took the road to the left, and that has made all the difference.

What did he hope to accomplish by this choice? In his own words from his Web site: "My hope for *The Da Vinci Code* was, in addition to entertaining people, that it might serve as an open door for readers to begin their own explorations and rekindle their interest in topics of faith." But explorations of what? Causing people to rekindle their interest in faith sounds like a noble cause. But since the book's release in 2003, we've heard no news stories of libraries overflowing with people coming to research what they read to find out if it was true. Instead, we have been bombarded with stories of people who are only too willing to take Dan Brown at his word and assume, like the *New York Daily News*, that "his research is impeccable!"

Well, we're going to peck a little.

Dan Brown didn't open a door for people to explore their faith. He opened a door to *heresy*, a word we'll talk about in more detail later. He didn't just open that door; he decorated it, made it more attractive. Behind door number one is everything your parents, your Sunday school teacher, and the Bible ever told you. Behind door number two is a total denial of Christian teachings. And behind Dan Brown's door number three (ta-da!) is a casual, stylish, don't-call-me-an-unbeliever heresy that doesn't seek to be verified or falsified, but begs to be chatted about over cocktails.

But why did *The Da Vinci Code* find us all so ready to accept that everything we've ever learned from trusted sources could no longer be trusted? And why were so many of us so willing to throw out previous teachings without even thinking it through first? Were we so desperate to abandon ship that we just needed someone to give us permission? Did we believe Brown when he told us that the only true enemy of religion is apathy and that controversy is actually good for us? (Try telling that to the Catholic Church.)

Or had postmodern relativism so infiltrated our culture by the time Brown's novel hit the shelves that we no longer even cared to differentiate between truth and fiction? Let's take a look at what was happening around the time *The Da Vinci Code* was released and explore some of the common themes among Brown's writings as a whole.

Troublesome Times, Troublesome Tale

The summer of 2003 was an odd time. History will remember the record-breaking heat waves that swept across much of Europe. The United States was busily engaged in the war on terror. The descendents of Thomas Jefferson's slave Sally Hemings gathered for a family reunion at Monticello. The election of an openly gay Episcopal bishop in New Hampshire threatened to split the worldwide Anglican Communion. And a book by a former English teacher from New Hampshire found its way onto millions of people's summer reading list.

Dan Brown's blockbuster *The Da Vinci Code* is an ingenious story. Starting with a murder at the Louvre in Paris in which the dying man arranges his own body as a clue that only protagonist Robert Langdon, a Harvard professor of religious symbology, will be able to decipher. (Despite its literary shortcomings, you do have to respect a book that casts a professor of religious symbology in the role of action hero.)

The deceased is renowned museum curator Jacques Sauniere. Using his own blood as ink and his abdomen as canvas, Sauniere has drawn five straight lines intersecting to form a five-pointed star—no small feat for a man who has been mortally wounded and is bleeding to death. Of course, Langdon immediately recognizes the symbol as a pentacle, "one of the oldest symbols on earth. Used over four thousand years before Christ" (*The Da Vinci Code*, 35).

The French police inspector assumes the pentacle represents devil worship. No, Langdon explains, that is a gross misperception, the product of Hollywood's imagination. "The pentacle is a pre-Christian symbol that relates to Nature worship. The ancients envisioned their world in two halves—masculine and feminine. Their gods and goddesses worked to keep a balance of power. Yin and yang. When the male and female were balanced, there was harmony in the world. When they were unbalanced, there was chaos. The pentacle is representative of the female half of all things— a concept religious historians call the 'sacred feminine' or 'the divine goddess.'"

Not only has the deceased drawn a pentacle on his belly, but, in what has to be the busiest death scene ever written, he has taken his clothes off and positioned his corpse in pentacle form, per Leonardo's famous drawing, *The Vitruvian Man*. Clearly, there are deep mysteries afoot here.

The late curator Sauniere has left other clues that are even more perplexing (a workaholic, even in his death). But before Robert Langdon can investigate, he must first escape the clutches of the French police who figure him as the murderer. Enter beautiful young Sophie Neveu, granddaughter of the deceased. Ms. Neveu befriends Langdon and offers to facilitate his getaway. Before leaving the museum, however, they must first check out the *Mona Lisa*. Well, of course. And here is where the book takes one of its many excursions into the arcane.

Langdon tells Sophie that the Egyptian god of fertility was called Amon. The Egyptian goddess of fertility was Isis, which in ancient pictograms reads "L'isa." Put them together, and you get "Amon L'isa." Move one letter, and you get "Mona Lisa." (We moved a few more letters, and got "So Animal," but that's just weird and won't sell any books.)

It has been often noted that Mona Lisa is not particularly beautiful. But not until now have we known why. Langdon explains that Leonardo painted an androgynous self-portrait—equal parts male and female. "And that," he says, "is Da Vinci's little secret, and the reason for Mona Lisa's knowing smile" (*DVC*, 121). Forget the fact that most art historians (including the ones at the Louvre) believe this is a portrait of a  real woman, Lisa Gherardini, wife of Francesco del Giocondo. If it wasn't already, it now becomes clear that Brown is less interested in actual history and more interested in presenting his agenda.

Of more direct importance to our story, at the *Mona Lisa,* a clue leads Robert Langdon to the astonishing discovery that the dead man down the hallway, Sophie's grandfather, had been a member of the oldest surviving secret society on earth, the Priory of Sion, devoted to the sacred feminine, with an abiding contempt for the church. Langdon has written about this group. Leonardo served as grand master from 1510 to 1519. According to the novel, the list of past masters includes Renaissance artist Sandro Botticelli, scientist Isaac Newton, author Victor "Hunchback of Notre Dame" Hugo, and composer Claude Debussy—the elite of the artistic elite. None of this has ever been corroborated, but why bother with history now? Isn't it a fun ride?

"Sophie," says Langdon, "the Priory's tradition of perpetuating goddess worship is based on the belief that powerful men in the early Christian church 'conned' the world by propagating lies that devalued the female and tipped the scales in favor of the masculine.

"The Priory believes that Constantine and his male successors successfully converted the world from matriarchal paganism to patriarchal Christianity by waging a campaign of propaganda that demonized the sacred feminine, obliterating the goddess from modern religion forever."

Langdon educates Sophie on the Catholic Inquisition's 300-year campaign against "the dangers of freethinking women," identifying such as witches and burning them at the stake. (Never mind that there weren't any Catholics in Salem at the time of the Salem witch trials.) Today's world, Langdon suggests, is living proof of the success of said campaign.

"Women, once celebrated as an essential half of spiritual enlightenment, had been banished from the temples of the world. There were no female Orthodox rabbis, Catholic priests, nor Islamic clerics."

It takes a cool customer to offer such tutorials even as the French version of the FBI is combing the hallways of the Louvre looking for him. And, as the reader knows, the real killer is still out there—a giant albino monk (I am not making this up) bent on suppressing secrets that, if told, could be the undoing of the church.

Those attuned to contemporary Christian culture wars may have already noted that Sophie's name is itself a clue: "Sophie Neveu" is an anagram for "Wisdom New Eve." In the Greek version of the Old Testament book of Proverbs, the word we translate as "wisdom" was the word *Sophia,* suggesting a female quality to the wisdom of God. Recently, there has been a growing trend to "re-image" God in female form. Sophia serves as kind of a god created for women, by women. But do note that the idea of re-creating God in our image is usually considered anathema in Christian circles.

Finally taking leave of the Louvre, Robert and Sophie wind up at the palace of an eccentric religious art historian who tells Sophie the key to the mystery is in Leonardo's *The Last Supper.* This eccentric religious art historian invites Sophie to look closely at the person seated at Jesus' right hand—the place of honor. "As she studied the person's face and body, a wave of astonishment rose within her. The individual had flowing red hair, delicate folded hands and the hint of a bosom. . . ." Sophie exclaims, "That's a woman!"

"That, my dear," says the eccentric religious art historian, "is Mary Magdalene."

Sophie turns. "The prostitute?"

Now the reader gets another lecture in revisionist church history. We learn that Jesus used to kiss Mary Magdalene on the mouth in front of the rest of the disciples, making them all jealous. So, once Jesus was out of the picture, they launched a smear campaign to wreck her reputation, portraying her as a whore so no one would let her be the leader of the group. Interesting? Yes. Historical? No.

One of the reasons for *this* book is that millions and millions of Americans in the summer of 2003, along with untold numbers around the world since, read the Dan Brown version of church history. In his telling, the books of the New Testament were selected by self-interested men for self-interested purposes, and the church has been involved in a 2,000-year conspiracy to suppress the writings that didn't toe the company line. As we shall see later (in chap. 5), this fits with Dan Brown's overall perspective on history.

Says the eccentric religious art historian in Brown's novel, "The modern Bible was compiled and edited by men who possessed a political agenda—to promote the divinity of the man Jesus Christ and use His influence to solidify their own power base."

Robert Langdon interjects, "An interesting note. Anyone who chose the forbidden gospels over Constantine's version was deemed a heretic. The word *heretic* derives from that moment in history. The Latin word *haereticus* means 'choice.' Those who 'chose' the original history of Christ were the world's first *heretics*."

If by "original history of Christ" one means the notion that Jesus was not God in the flesh living a sinless life and dying on the cross to pay the price for the sins of the world, then, yes, these were the world's first heretics. But the word *haereticus* doesn't just mean "choice" or "able to choose." Its original meaning also carries the notion of being factious.

Granted, in a year when former senator Frank Keating, a man handpicked by Roman Catholics to lead the inquiry into the church's role in sheltering pedophilia among priests, resigned after saying his experience was like dealing with the Mafia, it will be easy for many to believe the historic church is just one big organized crime syndicate. Dan Brown certainly believes that. And, apparently, so do millions of others.

Setting Up the Straw Man

The Roman Catholic Church is the New York Yankees of the religious world. They've been around so long, and they have all the money and all the history on their side. Something in us respects that; something else in us suspects it, resents it, and really likes to root against it. We're a nation that cheers for the underdog, and the Holy Roman Catholic Church is clearly not the underdog. We're for simple folks from small towns, not educated Europeans from Vatican City.

America is a famously Protestant nation, and often Roman Catholics have been portrayed as the enemy. In politics, John F. Kennedy was elected only after he substantially repudiated his faith. He had to insist that he wouldn't live out his faith if elected—a compromise that perhaps should have disqualified him from being both a Catholic and a president.

Despite what Brown says in interviews, his novels are famously anti–Roman Catholic. And many people, horrified by scandal (pedophilia, corruption, etc.) in the church, are looking for some kind of release valve for their anger and disgust. Brown's novels helpfully serve such readers by publicly labeling Roman Catholicism as what many people privately believe it to be: a corrupt, untrustworthy, deceptive religious organization built on a history of disreputable and harmful hierarchy of misogynistic leaders. It's relatively easy to cast the Roman Catholic Church in the role of bad guys. And it's not too big a stretch to see them branding everyone who disagreed with them with a scarlet *H* for "Heretic."

But, while the word *heretic* has been misused in the past and continues to be misused today, we cannot dismiss it as easily as Dan Brown wants us to. It is a sad but true fact that we may be called heretical for disagreeing over a great many things—ordination of women, modes of baptism, our view of biblical prophecy. Unfortunately, the word *heresy* is often used to protect a base of power or some long-held dogma.

Sometimes, however, persons are called heretics because they actually *are* heretics. Dan Brown, Elaine Pagels (we'll get to her later), and those others who champion the Gnostic gospels (which Dan Brown has helped to popularize) are heretics, not simply because they choose to believe an alternative story of Jesus, but because they support a salvation-stopping falsehood while creating division and attitudes of superiority among academia and the cheap-thriller readers.

Thriller

The Da Vinci Code is a fast-paced, put-your-brain-in-park page-turner that hasn't a well-turned phrase or a well-rounded character. So why would 40 million people read it? How could a forty-year-old school teacher gain credit for "no less than keeping the publishing industry afloat"[1] and for almost single-handedly causing a rush of tourism all over Europe and a new passion (albeit uninformed) for art and history?

Maybe everyone was just crazy from the heat. Perhaps they were bleary-eyed from having been glued to CNN every waking moment since 9/11. Perhaps the religious and historical scandals of the day finally created an insatiable thirst for conspiracy theories, and postmodern relativism swung the doors wide open. What we can say for sure is that people weren't reading Dan Brown's book because it is a literary masterpiece—because it's not.

And neither are any of the other Dan Brown novels that made a rip-roaring comeback the year *The Da Vinci Code* headed toward shattering sales records. "Pretty impressive," said Michelle Orecklin in the previously mentioned *Time* article, "given that the New Hampshire native's three previous works barely caused a ripple and, strictly speaking, the novel is heretical. It's perhaps worth noting that one of the very few books to sell more copies than *The Da Vinci Code* in the past two years is the Bible."

Had Brown's writings emerged 100, 50, or even 20 years ago, it is likely he would never have been published. Literary critics would have thought his books to be contrived and thin. With two-dimensional characters and highly improbable action, they are the stuff of dime-store pulp fiction, even comic books.

But in the summer of 2003, readers wanted something different—no Tolstoy, Hemingway, or even Mark Twain. They wanted an escape, and Dan Brown was happy to oblige. *The Da Vinci Code* sparked interest in Brown's former books (Brown's Web site reports that in early 2004, *The Da Vinci Code, Angels and Demons, Deception Point,* and *Digital Fortress* all held spots on the *New York Times* bestseller list simultaneously), which espouse similar philosophies; and, like lemmings, we've slipped down a fast-paced, entertaining cliff.

The problem is in the pace. Once you've put your brain in park and committed to a joy ride, you don't expect to have to get up and do research. It's fiction, right? And once our sexy heroes have awakened to a phone call that sweeps them away in a race against the clock to expose the authority-figure-institution gone bad, we're hooked.

And we—who have a hard time keeping up when our favorite blogger writes more than 200 words, who prefer our news in headlines and sound bites—we love Dan Brown's short chapters. They are short enough to be read at a stoplight or a lunch break. Though they're predictable and stilted, we somehow feel compelled to follow these storylines through until the mystery is solved. It is so easy to get sucked in. And when we realize how easy it was to finish the first Brown book, it's tempting to go out and pick up another.

The tragic result? Millions of people who have read Dan Brown's books have unwittingly imbibed his philosophy and worldview as well. Don't believe it? Just last month a friend of ours met a stranger in the airport. This stranger wanted to have an intellectual discussion about the falsities of historic Christianity based on one book: You guessed it—*The Da Vinci Code*. Our friend recognized the quotes from Dan Brown and called the stranger on it, but the stranger held his ground. It was shaky ground, but he held to it. It is situations like this that have led us here. We'll start the research for you. All you have to do is read. But please, we encourage you not to become guilty of ignorant acceptance as was the stranger at the airport. Go check it out for yourselves. We urge you to do so. By engaging yourself in seeking the truth, you will open a door to real faith, and that will make all the difference.

Chapter 2

WHAT MIGHT HAVE BEEN?

*D*uring the peak of Dan Brown's popularity, two landmark events occurred, which some have suggested had the potential to spark another great awakening: The release of Rick Warren's *The Purpose-Driven Life* and the release of Mel Gibson's *The Passion of the Christ.* The monumental success of these two works stoked an already huge and growing national interest in spiritual issues that seems to have dawned with the new millennium.

Even before the events of 9/11, Bruce Wilkinson's *The Prayer of Jabez* was flying off the shelves, eventually selling more copies in a single year than any other book in American publishing history. Authors like Lee Strobel and Ravi Zacharias produced well-researched books on apologetics that actually sold well. Authors like Max Lucado and Joyce Meyer had books being sold in nontraditional stores like Wal-Mart. Authors like John Ortberg and Philip Yancey were making good Christian literature more accessible to common readers. Many churches were seeking to become more relevant and reach people the church, as a whole, had ignored for years. Many Christians were taking seriously the charge to love God with their minds.

In the months and then years after one of the most tragic events in the history of our country, it became increasingly clear that people were yearning for something transcendent, something deeply spiritual. Faced with the uncertainty of our world and with the reality of their own mortality, people began gravitating towards the spiritual to seek out answers to the questions that have bothered humanity for millennia. Who are we? Why are we here? What's wrong with our world? Is there a solution to the problems that confront us? These are the issues that Rick Warren, Bruce Wilkinson, Mel Gibson, and others attempted to speak to with their respective works.

Both general bookstores and Christian bookstores reported an increase in sales after September 11, 2001: "The impact of Sept. 11 on our culture and on our industry cannot be overstated," said Bill Anderson, president of the Christian Booksellers Association (CBA). And in a single day in September 2001, Zondervan reported shipment of $1 million in Bibles, double the normal sales volume for that time of year—making September 2001 the second biggest revenue month in the seventy years of Zondervan's history.[1]

You'd think some sort of awakening was about to happen, what with all those Christian books and Bibles being sold. You'd think, at least, that something was going to happen—if not an all-out revival, perhaps some kind of Christian intellectual renaissance. All this while, between 1991 and 2004, the number of adults who don't attend church nearly doubled.[2] Something was going on.

First Bishop T. D. Jakes and then Rick Warren was dubbed "America's Pastor." Was our country coming together behind some notable Christian leaders in a full-blown rebuilding of a faithful nation? Hundreds of churches all over the country worked their way through "40 Days of Purpose" campaigns, thousands of people came to church and Christ for the first time, experiencing what Brian MacQuarrie of the *Boston Globe* called a "seismic shakeup."[3] It looked like the same people who left the church disillusioned and bitter after the scandals that rocked both Catholic and Evangelical worlds in the early '90s were coming back to Jesus. But they remained skeptical about his church.

So when people left the theater after *The Passion* or finished their forty-day study and went back to Barnes and Noble for another book about Jesus, they were greeted by kiosks of Dan Brown books being pushed as spiritual literature.

Can we really fault Dan Brown as the source for sidetracking an entire population and bringing a national revival to a halt? Probably not, but the timing certainly was interesting. People who left their faith behind realized that when catastrophe happens, the desire to cling to a transcendent God resurfaces. Yet, given their distaste for the pseudo-community most churches have to offer, they wanted Christianity without the church. Dan Brown was more than happy to oblige.

We can add to the guilty parties the media, like ABC, with their irresponsible reporting of historic events in their special "news presentation," *Jesus, Mary and Da Vinci* (note the not-so-subtly deceptive subtitle), *The Truth Behind the Mystery*. Of course, this "news presentation" proved to be about as anticlimactic as Geraldo Rivera's infamous broadcast, *The Mystery of Al Capone's Vault*. Not one credible scholar was produced who could verify Dan Brown's claims. Even Elaine Pagels, a fervent supporter of the unsubstantiated Gnostic gospels, suggested that all of it is based on speculation.

Yet, what were people to think? How were they to uncover the truth? What happens when a biblically and historically illiterate culture is hit head-on by Gnosticism masquerading as enlightenment and a postmodern denial of absolute truth masquerading as tolerance? And how will we recover from this collision?

Let's Go Slowly Here

These days, religion is out, but spirituality is in. And since 9/11, more people are seeking to find meaning and purpose in their lives. The problem comes when we pick through our "spiritual options" and build our belief systems like a Subway sandwich ("I'll have some Christianity on that, please. But hold the history. Oh, and sprinkle on some Eastern Mysticism"). Ideas have histories, and we would do well to discover what those are before swallowing them whole. Let's talk about some of the ideas mentioned in the last paragraph.

First, there's Gnosticism. The Microsoft Word autocorrect function catches it every time we type it, capitalizing the first letter. You may not recognize it so quickly, but after we explain a bit, you should start to recognize where it's snuck into our culture.

Gnosticism is a heresy that's about 1,800 years old. It showed up just as eyewitnesses to Jesus' ministry, death, and resurrection were dying out. If one person said, "Well, Jesus used to teach that the earth is flat," there was no one who could say with the authority of an eyewitness, "He did not!"

Gnosticism isn't about a flat earth. But it is about earthly things versus spiritual things. Gnostics believed that all things fell into one of two categories: matter or spirit. Further, they believed that all matter was evil (having been created by an evil deity), and all things spiritual were good (having been created by a good—but unknowable—god). A human person, according to this thinking, was a spirit caught up in an evil body on an evil planet governed by an evil god. The only way out was by an ecstatic spiritual experience in which the Gnostic was able to climb into the heavenlies, find a spirit guide, and dodge the bad spirits attempting to keep him/her out of there.

This all sounds a bit like a video-game, but there are people who really believed this. They believed the more of these experiences they had, the more knowledge they gained. Those who had more of this knowledge were superior to other believers. And all these self-proclaimed superior people were among the ranks of Christians in the second century. This Gnosticism, of course, affected their Christianity. Was Jesus fully divine? If so (by Gnostic thinking), then he could not have been fully human. He couldn't have had an actual physical body, because bodies are made of matter, which is inherently evil. But humans have bodies. If Jesus was divine, he couldn't have been human. So they believed that Jesus was a spirit, an apparition. This is a heresy called *Docetism*.

Others believed he really was human. But if he was human, then he would have been evil, and good cannot also be evil. These folks concluded that Jesus was a man, but when he was baptized, the spirit of "the Christ" descended upon him and stayed with him until right before he was crucified. Jesus the man died, but the Christ spirit lived on. This heresy is called *Adoptionism*.

Some still believe in Gnosticism in one form or another, though they may have modified it some. And it is the writings of a group of these Gnostic intellectuals that serve as the foundation for *The Da Vinci Code* and *Angels and Demons*. These "scholars" are generally dismissed by the majority of true academicians as . . . well, crackpots. Still, Gnosticism is gaining in popularity among feminists and others.

And though this growing group of people, hungry for spiritual things, seeks determinedly after answers, they don't always seek after those answers very wisely. In a culture that throws off authority, who do you ask for help when you're looking for the truth? Brown asked the Gnostics, and they led him to tell people that you can't trust the church.

So after the Roman Catholic guy's movie and the evangelical guy's book, if people read the Gnostic guy's book, what are they supposed to think? We're all taught from childhood that the truth usually lies somewhere in the middle. So maybe we should take some of Mel Gibson's movie, mix in some of Rick Warren's catchy slogans, and sprinkle liberally with Dan Brown's revisionist history.

This is what passes for enlightenment these days.

We'll get to the philosophy of postmodernism (as well as its tenet of tolerance) in the next chapter, but let's move now to some other reasons why a revival might have been interrupted.

Fighting "Bad Religion"

As mentioned in chapter 1, the state of the Roman Catholic Church was a contributing factor to the success of Dan Brown's novel and perhaps to the inability of the church, as a whole, to reach the public effectively in the aftermath of 9/11. While we evangelicals understand clearly the difference between Catholicism and Protestantism, the average unchurched person does not.

Brown's book blurs the lines even further. Unfortunately, the "organized church" gets hit with accusations all the time. Brown uses it as a punching bag. "Religion," he says, is bad. Not Christianity? No, over and over in *The Da Vinci Code* and *Angels and Demons*, we're told that "religion" is the enemy of science, scientific progress, the original history of Jesus, and the equal treatment of women in society. But Dan Brown doesn't mean Islam, does he? If so, he never mentions any examples from Islam. He doesn't mean to say that Judaism impedes the progress of science, does he? And what about Buddhism or Hinduism? Are those part of the "religion" that he says is so harmful and destructive to our world?

No, it's clear what he means. He means Roman Catholicism—consistently, and without exception. Why? It might just be because it's simpler that way. It's easier to set up one straw man and knock him down repeatedly than to face what's really there. That's the most charitable guess we could make: one church, one heap of great crimes against humanity. It makes for easier writing and easier reading. Not more truthful writing and reading. Not writing that's more faithful to the complexities of real life and real history. That would be much harder to do than pulling out stock villains in flowing robes and funny hats, toting suitcases full of money. According to Dan Brown, Catholics are "religion." They are "the church," the only Christians in the world.

This from a man who claims to have spent six years researching his book.

Putting the Fire Out

So did this accusation of "bad religion" have anything to do with dousing a fire of revival? When people finished *The Da Vinci Code* and went back and read Brown's *Angels and Demons, Digital Fortress,* and *Deception Point,* did that just solidify Brown's impact on American culture? If it hadn't been for the success of *The Da Vinci Code,* few people would have even known those other books existed. Now they are on best-seller lists, being lauded as master thrillers—poorly written as they are.

Still, no one ever went broke underestimating the taste of American readers. What is amazing, however, is the American public's ability to read two conflicting books and never think twice about it.

Case in point: Rick Warren's *Purpose-Driven Life* was released in October 2002 and spent about two years on the *New York Times* best-seller list. Think that through for a moment. *The Da Vinci Code* and *The Purpose-Driven Life* have both been on the best-seller list for about the same amount of time at almost exactly the same time. Clearly, there was overlap. Many of the same folks who had Rick Warren's book on their nightstand were reading Dan Brown's book on the airplane. And a lot of these were the same people who made Mel Gibson's *The Passion of the Christ* one of the biggest box-office hits of all time.

Jesus Who?

Could there be any kind of connection between these three cultural juggernauts? Yep, Jesus. Jesus is popular. People love Jesus. They just don't like church, and they really don't like Christians. They don't like people to ask them to use their discernment. But they love Jesus. And all three of these things have Jesus in great supply.

The problem is, which Jesus is the right Jesus?

Throughout the centuries, people have debated the meaning of the word *gospel*. Obviously, it literally means "good news," but what exactly is the good news that Christianity offers? To some extent, the answer to that question depends on who you ask. For example, the gospel according to Jesus seems to be "The kingdom of God is at hand." The gospel according to Paul differed slightly: "Jesus came and died and rose from the dead so we can be reconciled to God." The gospel according to Martin Luther was "By faith alone are we justified." The gospel according to Mel Gibson is "Jesus suffered and died so we can have eternal life." The gospel according to Rick Warren is "Jesus restores us to God so we can have a purposeful life."

So what is the gospel according to Dan Brown? Simply put, "Everything you've ever heard about Jesus is wrong."

And this is good news for whom?

Feeding the Suspicion

In an age of thriving interest in conspiracy theories, there is a pervading assumption that institutions don't communicate truth, and they often conspire to hide it—an assumption that Dan Brown's novels feed and fatten. Brown taps into the public's present fascination with religious esoterica and the occult, conspiracy theories, basic anti-Roman Catholic clericalism, the postmodern hermeneutic of suspicion, and the interest of those who want to know the "true" (read "new" and mainly "false") origins of Christianity.

Ultimately, one thing that Rick Warren, Mel Gibson, and Dan Brown all share is that they promise answers to difficult questions. That is undeniably attractive. At least with the first two, the answers are based on historical events. Dan Brown's answers are based on wild speculations and fringe scholarship. Yet people accept his theories as fact because he has told them to. On the very first page of *The Da Vinci Code* he states, "FACT: . . . all descriptions of artwork, architecture, documents, and secret rituals in this novel are accurate."

In an interview with Barnes and Noble, he declared: "One of the many qualities that makes *The Da Vinci Code* unique is the factual nature of the story. All the history, artwork, ancient documents, and secret rituals in the novel are accurate—as are the hidden codes revealed in some of da Vinci's most famous paintings."

In a page posted on his official Web site, Brown lists a number of completely (and provably) false statements, but titles them "Bizarre True Facts from DVC." This particular Internet page by Brown actually quotes from a document known as *Les Dossiers Secrets*, which was found in Paris' Bibliotheque Nationale. According to Brown, it proves that members of the super-secret Priory of Sion organization included Leonardo da Vinci, Botticelli, and Sir Isaac Newton. But *Les Dossiers Secrets* is nothing but a forgery penned in the 1960s by a French con man (Pierre Plantard, whom we'll discuss later) and deposited in the Paris Library. Although such information is widely known and accepted in France and throughout Europe, most Americans are still in the dark about Brown's sources. And this ignorance has made Brown a millionaire.

Marketing Mania

Brown's publisher, Doubleday, has only made things worse by lending their voice of support for claims that Brown's book is true. Stephen Rubin, president/publisher at Doubleday, has boldly stated that "John Grisham teaches you about torts. Tom Clancy teaches you about military technology. Dan Brown gives you a crash course in art history and the Catholic Church."[4] Such an assertion is terrifically irresponsible, given the fact that Brown is not qualified to speak on either subject and blatantly misrepresents verifiable aspects of art history and Roman Catholicism.

It would be nice if Dan Brown and Doubleday representatives would stick to saying, "It's only fiction." But they don't. They're saying that it is a fact-based book, containing true history and accurately representing a variety of historical events (e.g., the development of early Christianity, the original teachings of Jesus, the formation of the Bible, the artwork of Leonardo da Vinci, etc.). If Dan Brown and Doubleday had begun by clarifying that *The Da Vinci Code* was totally fiction, our book would not be necessary. But then maybe their book wouldn't have sold so well.

Saying that Dan Brown's book is about Christianity is like saying *Finding Nemo* is about marine biology. We have just as much evidence to suggest that Jesus was married to Mary Magdalene as we have that clown fish talk.

The Fiction the World Believes

Consider *Uncle Tom's Cabin*. Readers had to remind themselves that the book was fiction. But it wasn't "just" fiction. *Schindler's List* was fiction. But it wasn't "just" fiction. *Inherit the Wind* was fiction, but it wasn't "just" fiction. In fact, *Inherit the Wind* was fiction based on a factual event, but most people don't remember the actual event anymore (the Scopes Monkey trial). Instead, they remember the *Inherit the Wind* version of that actual event. Likewise, there are people now who no longer remember the actual events of Jesus' life. They will now remember the Dan Brown version of the actual event. Think we're overstating the case? Think people aren't that gullible? Hang on until the next chapter.

Interestingly, despite Dan Brown's claims that "all the history" in the novel is "accurate," the copyright page of *The Da Vinci Code* actually explains in small print that "all of the characters and events in this book are fictitious, and any resemblance to actual persons, living or dead, is purely coincidental."

So which is it?

In the chapters that follow, we will explore Dan Brown's worldview to hone the discernment of Christians and perhaps put us back on the track toward that revival.

In a December 2003 article in *The National Review*, David Klinghoffer stated, "If I were a Christian . . . I would find it a little disturbing that some fellow Christians do in fact view this novel as a threat to their faith." He adds, "If the professional educators were doing their job, any believing Catholic past elementary-school age would know that Brown's book is a total falsehood."

Maybe another great awakening wasn't coming. But Dan Brown's writings have certainly diverted our attention, damaged our reputation, and disillusioned many honest and well-intentioned people.

Recovering

Recovery is difficult—especially as it entails starting with a deficit. While God is victorious—the Bible promises that—the church may not always be viable. In fact the Bible warns the church not to lose its ability to connect with the surrounding culture (1 Cor. 10:32–33). To stave off that day, Christians must fight against being fooled by the likes of Dan Brown.

Chapter 3

NAILING JELL-O TO A TREE

All the time the joke is that the word "mine" in its fully possessive sense cannot be uttered by a human being about anything. In the long run either [Satan] or [God] will say "mine" of each thing that exists, and specially of each man.
— C. S. Lewis, *The Screwtape Letters*

*I*t's an expression used to describe things that are nearly impossible: trying to understand teenagers, planning an election, finding a good spouse—anything that evades our grasp just as we think we've gotten our arms around it. But hey, we think, it never hurts to try. Get out your hammer, a nail, your favorite flavor of gelatin, and find the nearest tree. *Knock, knock, knock . . . FLOP.*

Understanding the postmodernism that dominates our culture is about as easy as nailing Jell-O to a tree. Any attempt to understand it, boil it down, or really define it will usually leave you with Jell-O on your shoes. Embracing this indefinable worldview actually seems more challenging than rejecting it. But many people do embrace it without having given it a lot of thought. At its heart, postmodernism claims that objectivism—the belief that truth and values exist independently of our perception of them or belief in them—is an outdated, unrealizable ideal. Not only is God dead, but truth itself is on life-support. And we often find ourselves debating whether to pull the plug.

But how can we tell people that Jesus is the Truth, if people no longer believe truth even exists? That's the dilemma Dan Brown speaks to. The truth is out there; it just doesn't look like anything you've ever seen before.

Everyone in our society has been influenced, to some extent, by postmodern relativism—even Christians. It is the postmodern philosophy that says, "It may be truth for you, but it's not truth for me." Such a philosophy allows Dan Brown to write things that are simply untrue but forbids anyone the right to correct him. Fundamental to accepting postmodernism is accepting, even embracing, absolute relativism—a true oxymoron and the only absolute postmodernists will allow.

So when an author writes a book (fiction or not) that calls into question foundational, historic truths and hands it to a generation like this one, a majority of people are willing to agree that this new version of truth is just as valid as the old version. At least that's what postmodernism says. As for how postmodernists behave, most will say that all truth claims are equally valid but will show preference to one viewpoint over another—usually the viewpoint that most readily justifies a laissez-faire approach to ethics and morality.

Regardless of what section Brown's book may sit in at Borders, there are people who will embrace the work as truth because of the mighty claim of "research" in the author's forward. And when we say "people," we're not talking about a few dozen oddballs.

If you go to Amazon.com, you'll see review after review saying things like the following:

> With his impeccable research, Mr. Brown introduces us to aspects and interpretations of Western history and Christianity that I, for one, had never known existed . . . or even thought about. I found myself, unwillingly, leaving the novel, and time and time again, going online to research Brown's research— only to find a new world of historic possibilities opening up for me. And my quest for knowledge and the answers to questions that the book poses, paralleled, in a sense, the quest of the book's main characters.

Is what The Da Vinci Code *proposes true? Well, the research is correct. The historical events and people explored in the book are real. But no one knows the Truth . . . nor will we ever, probably. I think that some things are meant to be a mystery. With all the world's diverse religions and each individual's belief in what is Divine, the Truth would have to destroy the beliefs, hopes and lives of many of the world's population. So, perhaps, in the divine scheme of things, there are many more Truths than one.*

I was not brought up in a religious house so I have always been a little skeptical when it comes to church doctrine. This is why I found this book so appealing, it gave me the Reader's Digest version of church history and the controversy that surrounds it.

I know a lot of Bible thumpers and Catholic sheep didn't like this book because it actually made sense, but to a person that is willing to go out of the ordinary and maybe even think for themselves, this book is a mindsaver! If you have an open mind and are at least a little bit intelligent, you will love this book. Not only does it have a great plot, it is more of a learning experience than most history books will teach you.

This book really opened my eyes about religion. I was raised as Roman Catholic (for 30 years), still believe in Jesus, etc. . . . but I have to say after reading this book and checking facts, I am starting to question the teachings of the church.

What would be so bad about Jesus being married anyway? Mohammed was married, you know! And what's more, this book shows up just how arrogant and bigoted Christianity is because it focuses on the man and the male. What's so wrong about female divinity anyway? Dan makes a very good point, amongst many others, that the Bible was written by humans, and what's more MALE humans. Of course it is going to reflect the interests of the church and the power it wielded over people!

I strongly urge everyone to read this book. It is guaranteed to make you think twice about some things in the future, and make you look at things in a whole new light. You will probably find yourself looking up things online to see if they're true, and then find yourself amazed when you reveal the truth and you realize Dan Brown knows his stuff.

If you don't think for yourself, don't bother with this intellectually and spiritually challenging work by Dan Brown. This book is a highly provocative mind-opener, so you really have to be a courageous, free-thinking person in order to really get into it and explore new territory. It throws into question many of our comfortable traditions and truisms, our cherished and well-defended beliefs and practices (like going to church every Sunday and trusting the clichés coming from the pulpits above us). I believe that this novel is a landmark on our journey toward greater self-awareness and freedom of intellectual exploration—but you have to be gutsy enough to shed a lot of mental baggage and inherited illusions to get there. If you want to be brave and expand your consciousness, read this work. If you want to remain a sheep amongst the flock with the same color of wool over your eyes, then do not even venture into the first chapter. It will shake you to the foundations of your uncritical thought. Stay where you are. Pray. Snooze. Follow the dicta and the routines of your church. The pure sunlight out here in Dan Brown-land can be blinding, especially for sheep.

Even if it were a story with ideas and theories that are completely made up, it would still be great. However the fact that all the information in it is TRUE, makes it all that *much better. A lot of hardcore Christians are screaming for this book's demise, but that would be beneficial to no one. I'll say it right now, that I would probably classify myself as one of those "Hardcore Christians," and yet I found this book just amazing. If anything, one of the messages of the book is the reinforcement of there being a God. It simply states that the Bible we read and the things we are taught represent those thoughts and ideas CHOSEN FOR US TO THINK, by people in power thousands of years ago. Example. Did you know there were originally some 80 gospels? Not just the four from Matthew, Mark, Luke, and John that we have been told? Before reading this book I was not aware of that at all.*

On and on they go—nearly 4,000 of them. We've included a large sampling to show that it's not just a handful of people buying into this; it's hundreds and thousands, perhaps millions of people being fooled by the pseudo-scholarship of Dan Brown. Good people have been duped. Mean people have been given ammunition. Well-meaning Christians have come across looking like ostriches with their heads in the sand or, worse, just as mean-spirited as the hardcore atheists who post their arguments with smugness and arrogance.

Dan Brown is one postmodernist whose relativism has had such an influence on so many people's thinking that large numbers of his readers are actually abandoning a historical understanding of truth.

Redefining Tolerance

Recently, relativists have gained a wider audience by disseminating a new definition of the word *tolerance*. Previous generations defined tolerance as simply accepting the existence of differences between individuals in their thinking—agreeing to disagree. Citizens and nations should have the legal freedom to practice the religion of their choice; we should universally show respect to others, even if we think their beliefs are wrong. It is tolerant to tell people you think their beliefs are wrong; it is intolerant to tell people that they should not be allowed to believe wrong things. Tolerance implies disagreement and a belief that one opinion more closely corresponds to reality than another. There has always been and should always be room for tolerance and differences of opinion in matters of taste.

Today's tolerance, however, goes beyond accepting another person's right to be wrong and says that we must embrace the other person's position as if it were just as true as ours. When discussing tolerance today, it means never, ever calling others' beliefs false or untrue. If you do, you are a conceited, prejudiced, intolerant extremist. Tolerance is no longer accepting someone else's right to be wrong; it is embracing their view and denying that there is such a thing as "wrong."

It is one thing to ask questions about the nature of the world or of ourselves—such as how old the earth is or whether human beings possess a soul. It is another thing altogether to ask questions about whether *any* questions about the world or people *can actually be answered*. We are now living in a culture that increasingly questions the whole idea of truth as an objective reality that is the same for all people and according to which all people must order their lives. This is a dangerous idea with dangerous consequences. And it has spawned several other, equally dangerous ideas with equally dangerous consequences.

Extremely Relative

As our society became more and more multicultural, people realized that not everyone sees and understands the world in the same way. Rather than using this as a catalyst for serious dialogue, society has merely accommodated everyone's view in a mishmash of validation. Instead of working to find agreement on the basis of transcendent values, values were simply abandoned in favor of the watered-down version of tolerance discussed above. So now no absolute reality exists; there are only varying constructions of reality that differ because of our different experiences, abilities, and conditions. And this belief gets incorporated into our public education system.

As long as a person's belief system is internally consistent, as long as it is not blatantly contradictory, we are supposed to embrace it and place it alongside our own. Well, that's the party line. The truth is, the very notion that all beliefs are equally valid is itself blatantly contradictory and an impossible philosophy to live by. Everyone has a moral hierarchy—even the relativist who prefers the ideas of other relativists to traditionalists.

Postmodern relativists consider themselves pragmatic: as long as your belief system allows you to get ahead and be successful, have at it. Who's to say you're wrong to believe what you believe—especially if you have all the money and power. Oops, there's another slip of moral hierarchy for relativists: success is preferred to failure. Is that considered to be some kind of self-evident truth?

We're allowed to ask if a person's perspective makes sense. And we're allowed to ask if it works. The one thing we're not allowed to ask is if it's true. The notion that we might want a perspective that actually corresponds to reality is considered meaningless. For postmodern relativists, the only thing that matters is the choice to embrace a worldview with no objective reality.

For relativists, all religions are equally true, and it is not possible for any to be wrong. If all religions are true, then it is impossible to make a mistake when choosing your religious allegiance, right? Well, then, why does Dan Brown go to such great lengths to show us such damning examples of things people have done for their religion: The Spanish Inquisition, the burning of "heretics" by the Roman Catholic Church, the subjugation of women. Clearly, many religious practices are objectively evil, but a true relativist cannot say that some are evil without borrowing from the Judeo-Christian philosophy. Theologian Daniel Clendenin says, "Simply put, consistent pluralism tolerates the intolerable."[1] It has to, or its message self-destructs.

Probably without considering the implications of such beliefs, some Christians like to be thought of as tolerant. That's why religious pluralism has become so fashionable of late. And because of it, people can make choices like those of one man we know who is immersed in a pagan lifestyle and rituals, believes in spirits, and communicates with them, while still maintaining his membership and involvement in a local Methodist church. He simultaneously claims to believe Hinduism and Christianity to be the same story because they both hold promise of redemption.

John 14:6 says, "I am the way and the truth and the life. No one comes to the Father except through me." Religious pluralism slams against this verse like a brick wall. Yet there are those who only know one definition of the word *tolerant* and believe that loving others as Jesus did means embracing their beliefs as well. Those with this mind-set feel generous when they say, "Chinese food or French cuisine, Jesus or Nostradamus, permed or straight, life or death: they are all the same. What you choose does not matter, only your freedom in choosing."[2]

As Christians, we should uphold legal and social tolerance to the highest standard, but this is not relativism. As Mortimer J. Adler said in *Truth in Religion*, there is always room for tolerance in matters of taste but not in matters of truth.[3] To embrace extreme relativism in the areas of truth, morals, and values is to reduce these areas to matters of taste. Moreover, if everything everyone believed was always true, what would the word *truth* mean? As Norman Geisler and Peter Bocchino say in *Unshakable Foundations*, "To point in every direction is the same as not to point at all!"[4]

The Bible is filled with many different religions. But it is also full of stories about Jesus, Paul, and many others who converted thousands of formerly deceived polytheists. Although it is clear that our world's understanding of religion has changed significantly, the same basic principles of salvation stand true: *Jesus is the way and the truth and the life. No one comes to the Father except through him.* This is the bedrock of our faith in Jesus Christ, and abandoning it is abandoning him.

The Importance of Living in History

Ann was named for her paternal grandmother. She lives within ten miles of her parents and three miles of her husband's parents, and both sides of the family attend church together. Her children know all of their cousins, and Christmas is a time to practice traditions that have been passed down for more than a century. Every other year, at a family reunion, distant family members come to her Georgia home and talk about the way things used to be. Someone gave her all the letters her grandparents wrote each other during World War II, which she hopes to have published one day. A family tree hangs framed in her hallway with her kids' names scribbled in at the bottom. She believes her purpose in life is to invest in her children, so they can be great people some day.

There was a time when people like Ann were not unusual. Ann lives, and loves living, within a continuity of culture—she lives rooted in history.

But few of us live like that anymore. During the 1970s, when the postmodern generation (sometimes called *GenX*) was being born and growing up, many things about family and life began to change. "The proportion of children living with their parents, which had remained stable at about 85 percent since 1880, began to slide. The divorce rate more than doubled."[5] This one factor alone, the breakdown of the family as the cornerstone of society, has made it much easier for traditional values to be marginalized in favor of "progressive enlightenment." We rarely ever go to Grandma's anymore to listen to stories of what life was like when she was our age. Instead, we go to Starbucks to sit among peers and pool our ignorance.

Not only have we lost the sense of our place in history, we've also lost religious knowledge. The general public is far more biblically illiterate than ever before. As George Lindbeck comments, "There was a time when every educated person, no matter how professedly unbelieving or secular, knew the actual text from Genesis to Revelation with a thoroughness that would put contemporary ministers and even theologians to shame."[6]

If people were biblically literate, Dan Brown's writings would not be so influential. Instead, the influence of our postmodern culture turns fact into fable and reality into fairy tale. Our culture is easily duped. As J. P. Moreland says in *Love Your God with All Your Mind,* "Because of the mindlessness of our culture, people do not persuade others of their views (religious or otherwise) on the basis of argument and reason, but rather, by expressing emotional rhetoric and politically correct buzzwords. Reason has given way to rhetoric, evidence to emotion, substance to slogan, the speech writer to the makeup man, and rational authority (the right to command compliance and to be believed) to social power (the ability to coerce compliance and outward conformance). Rhetoric without reason, persuasion without argument is manipulation."[7]

As Long as It Feels Good!

On his Web site, Dan Brown says that his hope in writing *The Da Vinci Code* was that the story would serve as a catalyst and a springboard for people to discuss the important topics of faith, religion, and history. Sadly, as the reviews from Amazon.com reveal, many have decided *not* to think through their beliefs; instead, they choose to embrace a warm, fuzzy pluralism and serve a fictionalized Jesus, all the time thinking they've gained some superior knowledge. Note Mr. Brown's Web site response to the question of if he is a Christian:

> *Yes. Interestingly, if you ask three people what it means to be Christian, you will get three different answers. Some feel being baptized is sufficient. Others feel you must accept the Bible as absolute historical fact. Still others require a belief that all those who do not accept Christ as their personal savior are doomed to hell. Faith is a continuum, and we each fall on that line where we may. By attempting to rigidly classify ethereal concepts like faith, we end up debating semantics to the point where we entirely miss the obvious—that is, that we are all trying to decipher life's big mysteries, and we're each following*

our own paths of enlightenment. I consider myself a student of
many religions. The more I learn, the more questions I have.
For me, the spiritual quest will be a life-long work in progress.

As intelligent, well-read, and prolific as he may be, Mr. Brown just dumped himself right into Moreland's category of reason giving way to rhetoric when he said that we are each following our own paths of enlightenment. *Knock, knock, knock—FLOP.* There goes the Jell-O. If you can't say, "No one can come to the Father except through Jesus," you aren't truly a Christian—no matter where you may stand on Brown's continuum.

Jell-O or Jesus?

First Chronicles 12:32 is a short verse that tells us of the men of Issachar, "who understood the times and knew what Israel should do." That's what we need. Instead of seeking out popular ideas, we need to be people who seek out the truth. We should strive to be "egalitarian about people and elitist about ideas," as Peter Kreeft says in *The Snakebite Letters.*[8] The fact is, we should be exclusive about some things. You may think it's a harmless philosophy, but trust us: there are some circumstances in which you don't want to encounter a postmodernist. For example, you want an absolutist for an auto mechanic. You do not want a mechanic who believes that water, oil, gas, and brake fluid are all a matter of preference.

Seriously, though, if we are Christians, there are absolutes to which we must cling. Jesus' saving work must be *known and embraced* for persons to be saved. Unfortunately, our culture has everything upside-down and has become elitist about people and egalitarian about ideas. In this environment, we must learn with certainty the traditional claims of Christianity and protect with conviction the objective and absolute truth.

The Christian faith claims to be the only appropriate form of faith. By its own declaration of absolute truth it casts a shadow of imperfect reality on every other system. Stephen Neill says, "This Christian claim is naturally offensive to the adherents of every other system. It is almost as offensive to modern man, brought up in the atmosphere of relativism, in which tolerance is regarded as the highest of the virtues. But we must not suppose that this claim to universality is something that can quietly be removed from the [g]ospel without changing it into something entirely different from what it is. The mission of Jesus . . . [does] not make sense unless interpreted in the light of his own conviction that he was in fact the final and decisive word of God to men."[9]

It is futile not only to try to *define* postmodernism, but also to live by it. Relativism fails its own test of plurality, because it claims that all religions are valid and that there are no absolutes. By claiming this, it becomes an absolute itself. *Knock, knock, knock—FLOP.* The Jell-O is in wiggly chunks at our feet. This is where Jesus takes the lead over gelatinous relativity, if you will. A poet once said it was not the nails that held Jesus to a tree, but his love. There we have an absolute. There we have three knocks that will hold to a tree. Absolute Jesus. Absolute love. Absolute truth.

Chapter 4

QUID EST VERITAS?

Luke, you're going to find that many of the truths we cling to depend greatly on our own point of view.
— Obi Won Kenobi in *The Return of the Jedi*

Quid est Veritas?" Perhaps the most notable question in the entire Bible comes from the lips of a Roman governor as he tries to determine what to do with Jesus. Pilate's question, "What is truth?" still rings loudly in our ears.

It is likely that Pilate's question had less to do with philosophical inquiry and more to do with political expediency. More than likely, he was asking Jesus, "Truth? What in the world does truth have to do with any of this mess we find ourselves in?"

After all, it is clear that the mob screaming for Jesus' blood was not interested in truth. It is equally clear that Pilate's judgment could not be based on the objective truth of the situation. His Roman superiors would not care that Jesus might actually have been innocent if a riot broke out during a Jewish holiday. Truth ought to be the deciding factor for the choices we make, but it rarely is.

It is Dan Brown's perspective on truth which guides his writing and fuels his apparent passion for conspiracy theories. But by embracing a relativistic worldview, Brown makes his claims nonfalsifiable. Unfortunately, it is impossible to contradict Dan Brown without being seen as a cultural elitist or claiming to be God. Or is it? We need to remember that Dan Brown's views may be nonfalsifiable, but they are also nonverifiable. We can make the choice *not* to believe everything he says.

As previously discussed, we live in a culture that has elevated tolerance above truth as a virtue. Our culture seeks to avoid being judgmental or closed-minded, instead affirming diversity and pluralism. In such a context, claims to truth (let alone absolute or objective truth) are regarded as backward and gauche.

But what about this claim—"You will know the truth, and the truth will set you free" (John 8:32)?

A Traditional View of Truth

Without a doubt, the most important issue that must be settled in contemporary society is the issue of truth. Many people now consider truth irrelevant, rejecting the notion of a universal or absolute truth. For them, truth is more of an opinion, and we all know that opinions are like noses: everybody has one. Your nose isn't my nose, and it needs to stay out of my face. Likewise, your truth isn't my truth and also needs to stay out of my face.

As we said before, there's plenty of room for tolerating differences in matters of opinion, but it's impossible to live like that in the arena of truth. For example, suppose you get a note from your bank telling you that you bounced a check. This should not have happened because you know you have plenty of money in the bank, so you call your bank to straighten things out. The person you speak to says, "Here's the problem: You wrote a check for $6,000, but you have only $300 in the account." You respond, "No, that's not true. I wrote a check for $600, and I have $3,000 in the account."

Imagine what you would do if the bank teller said, "Well, that may be true for you, but it's not true for me." Postmodernism sounds generous, until it starts messing with your bank balance.

The Christian truth claims that Dan Brown attacks are either true or false, not somewhere on a continuum. And truth is that which corresponds to reality, as God perceives it. Only God sees everything about everything.

In their book, *Unshakable Foundations*, Norman Geisler and Peter Bocchino call attention to just how much our thoughts shape the way we live: "Since our thoughts influence our emotions, reactions, and behaviors, it is particularly important for us to know what we believe and why we believe it." In the same book, they discuss "The Law of Non-Contradiction," which says that, logically, a thing cannot be *A* and *not A* at the same time. In other words, a fruit cannot be both an apple and an orange. A light cannot be both on and off at the same time. A person cannot be in Dallas and Atlanta at the same time. And a statement cannot be both true and false simultaneously. The idea that a belief can be true for you but not for someone else is absurd—it defies the definition of the words used and short-circuits our ability to communicate in meaningful ways.[1]

That's why an incoherent worldview should *not* be believed. In *No Doubt About It,* Winfried Corduan says that "a system containing inconsistent or contradictory statements at its core must be false."[2] To say that all religions are the same is nonsense. We don't mean that in a condescending way; we mean that in a technical and literal way: it does not make sense. If religions promote radically different ideas about what constitutes ultimate reality, the human condition, salvation, and ultimate destiny, someone's perspective is correct and someone else's is incorrect.

But there is another problem with the criteria for relativism (true only "for us"), subjectivism (true only because we feel it), and pragmatism (true because it works). If something is really true, it will be true regardless of whether people recognize it or not. And it will work because it is true, not *be true because it works*. If something is false, it is false regardless of how many people believe it. Truth is independent of the knower and his awareness. Truth isn't created; it is *discovered*.

Paul Copan has a wonderful example of the influence of truth "variants":

> *The person who is, say, the victim of torture, slave labor, child abuse, rape, or apartheid intuitively knows that justice is being violated. Are we really willing to concede that there is ultimately no significant moral difference between Hitler and Mother Teresa? Are we really willing to believe that genocide,*

rape, and murder are just "cultural" behaviors? The person who embraces moral relativism needs to be pressed: What if he were arrested and tortured for no reason? Why should he protest if you took a sledgehammer to his BMW? If he were a Jew in Nazi Germany, where the culture was horrifyingly anti-Semitic, why should his disagreement with the standards of the surrounding culture carry any weight at all? Why should his will be respected? After all, for someone who says, "Your values are true for you, but not for me," there can be no objectively morally degrading actions. Moral relativism is utterly unlivable.[3]

You might read this comment and think, "Hang on, that's talking about morality, not religion." But if our behaviors are shaped by our values and beliefs, there *is no separation,* and our worldview *is* our definition of truth, moral or otherwise. This example is not so far-fetched. Copan, a former associate of Ravi Zacharias International Ministries, has another work that is a helpful tool for Christians facing postmodern relativism: *True for Me, But Not For You: Deflating the Slogans That Leave Christians Speechless* (Bethany, 1998). In this book, he offers answers for Christians who find themselves bewildered by nonbelievers' statements of "All religions lead to God!" or "Christians are so intolerant." He reminds us that there will always be opposition to knowledge of truth, morality, the uniqueness of Christ, but that there is hope for those who have never heard the gospel. It is important to know how to answer the accusing questions and statements thrown at us, so that we will know how to maintain absolute truth, not just shy away, embarrassed, from its opposition.

Maintaining Truth

Spanish author Miguel de Unamuno wrote a book in 1931 that had a similar impact to Dan Brown's last two novels (though without the huge cash reward and with a great deal more style). In *San Manuel Bueno, martir,* Unamuno (who tried to believe in God and found he could not) claimed he was attempting to "shak[e] readers out of their complacency and forc[e] them to face the tragic contradictions of the human condition."[4] The book's writing predates postmodernism by decades, but it is interesting that Spain was, at the time, experiencing disillusionment with its leadership and a decline in life and culture that parallels that of America today.

The protagonist of Unamuno's book, Don Manuel, is vicar of a church in the quiet Spanish town of Valverde de Lucerna (green valley of light). He is an unbeliever who nonetheless wishes to preserve his flock from the faithlessness by which he himself is haunted. He delves into books to present a flawless dissertation of the gospel of Jesus, leaving his congregation breathless, deeply touched and maybe even changed. He spends time in the village going from home to home, blessing the families, working in their gardens, or just loving the children. The people adore him. He seems to be the ideal example of a man who can integrate scholarship and ministry in his life. But there is that one problem: he does not believe in God.

Why are we discussing an obscure European author who wrote more than seventy years ago? Because Unamuno, like Dan Brown, used his character to show that we fools who choose to believe don't really need a foundation for our faith. We just need the faith, and that makes us pathetic. Brown's game is not a new one. In *San Manuel Bueno*, Unamuno endeavors to undermine the faith of his readers, or at least to remove it from its foundations. He says he wants to shake readers out of complacency, but that's not exactly what he's doing (just like it's not to spark great discussions that Brown *really* writes his books). Instead, both of these authors attempt to destroy faith by making it look pitiable. As Dr. Rosemary Clark of Cambridge University said, Unamuno believed that "those who have been deluded into belief are in a fools' paradise and their awakening will be catastrophic."[5]

Like Brown, Unamuno plays with language to achieve his goals, like this translation he gives of 1 Corinthians 15:19: "If only for this life we have hope in Christ, we are to be pitied more than all men."

Well, are we miserable in this life if we choose to believe in something or someone we cannot see? We are if we don't seek to understand whether what we believe is objectively true. If our faith *is* a crutch (like so many unbelievers accuse), then we are to be pitied. But if our faith is an empowering force, based on texts that are historically reliable, and if it continues, the further we invest in it, to correspond with what we know is real *and* what works, we are in no fools' paradise.

But the response to Brown's books (and if you look on Amazon .com in the comments that follow *San Manuel Bueno, martir*, you'll see responses similar to those that follow Brown's books) makes one wonder how many carriers of the gospel find themselves hiding doubts and trying to protect themselves from their own uncertainty. What causes this faithless state of mind? Biblical illiteracy? A culture that denies absolutes? The apathy our culture exhibits and against which Unamuno was fighting so fiercely? People like Dan Brown? What laid the foundation for this tragedy?

Let's not assume this time that the answer lies simply in belief and unbelief, death and resurrection, or truth and falsehood. Instead, let's look at the tragic paradox of human personality, torn between a common-sense view of truth that claims a correspondence between what we claim to know and what actually is and an honest search that conforms our desires to truth, not truth to our desires. If God exists and speaks, his revelation would be objectively true, as it is the expression of a trustworthy person. This relates to the historical reliability and trustworthiness of Scripture too, but we'll get to that in a bit.

Nothing More; Nothing Less

The world is full of people who have embraced what philosophers call *naive realism*—a perception that the world is exactly as it appears, no more, no less. This perception is something like what a child believes when watching television before she can separate reality from fiction. If this perception doesn't have enough holes in it, try another school of thought, *subjective idealism*, an idea proposed by George Berkeley, an Irish philosopher in the eighteenth century. The idea here is that reality is made up of *only* mental objects, summarized in his maxim "Esse est percipi" (To be is to be perceived). In a nutshell, this is the idea that if we can't really know the *sense* and *emotional feeling* of an object, we can't really know it's real. Therefore, if we exist, it is because we think we do. Quick—for a minute, try thinking you don't exist. Anything happen? We didn't think so. This philosophy sounds ridiculous when you stop and think about it, but people are subscribing to it in droves.

Now let's examine Tom Wright's discussion of *critical realism* to gain a better understanding of this "correspondence" idea of reality. This theologian and Anglican Bishop of Durham says: "I propose a form of *critical realism*. This is a way of describing the process of 'knowing' that acknowledges the *reality of the thing known, as something other than the knower* (hence 'realism'), while fully acknowledging that the only access we have to this reality lies along the spiralling path of *appropriate dialogue or conversation between the knower and the thing known* (hence 'critical')."[6]

Now for a nice wrap-up of these philosophies of current thought.[7]

The Philosophy	In Our Own Words	School of Thought
Naïve realism	"There are balls and strikes, and I call them as they are."	Modernism
Subjective idealism	"There are balls and strikes, and they are what I call them."	Postmodernism
Critical realism	"There are balls and strikes, and I call them as I see them."	Correspondence

Again, the latter is a common-sense view of truth that claims a correspondence between *what we claim to know* and *what actually is*. This "dialogue" (as Wright calls it) is one that writers like Dan Brown have failed to have. It is the same thing that laid the foundation for Unamuno's tragedy. If we conduct an honest search that is consistent with our desire for truth, we will find it. But instead we tend to go with our own desires (good fiction, something that works for me, uh-oh things *aren't* working for me, if I believe this I don't have to ask questions anymore, etc.) and we end up with a "truth" that drives people away from common sense.

No Compromise! (What Not to Accept)

In the previously mentioned Hans Christian Andersen tale, *The Emperor's New Clothes,* counterfeit tailors take advantage of the emperor's tremendous fancy for the best and newest clothing. The tailors claim to make clothes that are invisible to all who are either unqualified for their position or very dim. But as the tale unfolds, we see the entire kingdom falling for the ruse, a band of crooks taking off with the jewels they procured for the garment, and a king walking around his entire village in the buff until a little child cries out the truth: the emperor isn't wearing anything. This story is the parable of our time. Even children know that some things are true and false, right and wrong, beautiful and ugly. Why do *we* refuse to believe it?

Even our educational system frequently relativizes the true, the good, and the beautiful and drives people away from common sense. One reason for this phenomenon is the fact that many thinking people use measures other than truth to deal with questions about truth. Peter Berger makes a similar claim in *The Precarious Vision:* "Perhaps the essential malady of these religious arguments is the attempt to use criteria other than truth in dealing with questions of truth. Perhaps this malady is the heart of religious bad faith. Whatever religious propositions we take, we confront thereby a burning question of truth. 'God exists'—yes or no? Is the statement true or is it not? No other criterion but that of truth respects the dignity of such a proposition."[8]

No other truth. God exists—or He does not.

We must refuse to let the voices of our culture steal from us what we know to be true ("Jesus is Lord"). We can't acquiesce to postmodern pickpockets who dupe us into thinking they are presenting truth just because so many others are accepting it.

A great number of people *are* affected by Brown's writings. But let these writings affect *us* in a different way. Let them inspire us to call out to everyone who will hear that the Emperor is exposed—and he is a pompous, naked king at that.

Truth for the Sake of the Kingdom

Along with the lack of continuity in our culture and ignorance of history and of biblical texts is the irresponsible way many churches have held to tradition. Traditions can be wonderful things. They can provide that desperately needed continuity and can help us build our faith. But there are those who continue in traditions that do not work and *do not* build faith.

Let us make a distinction between *tradition* and *traditionalism*. *Tradition* says the things we do are important because we've always done them; they are part of our identity, and they help us to grow closer to God. *Traditionalism* says the things we do are important because we've always done them. We don't care if they're not really working or may be causing our kids to turn their backs and walk out on church; we will keep doing them. (Of course, a good traditionalist would never put it that way.) It is this hard-nosed traditionalism that gives birth to the postmodern disrespect for truth. Traditionalism makes its children angry and turns people away from things that really are true.

Others of us have reacted to the traditionalism we've encountered by seeking change because we love change or because we hate what we've experienced. But the kingdom of God needs people who hold on to their traditions *and* seek change *for the sake of the kingdom.*

If we are to have an impact in our churches and the world, we must understand and maintain a traditional view of truth with humility, gentleness, and respect. These things are essential to civilized conversation with our postmodern friends. But being humble and respectful doesn't mean we have to accept ideas that cannot be proven. The burden of proof for the issues in *The Da Vinci Code* and *Angels and Demons* rests squarely on the shoulders of postmodern thinkers like Dan Brown, not on traditions that have been preserved for centuries (because the truth behind them has already been studied and found verifiable) for the sake of the kingdom of God.

Waiting for God

Samuel Beckett's play *Waiting for Godot* could be titled *Waiting for God.* The audience witnesses two men discussing their plight as they sit and wait for their respected Godot to show up. They analyze him to pieces until he does come. Then they miss him because he is unrecognizable to them. This is where the danger lies for truth-seekers who put their faith in what is truly only postmodern fiction. The people of Valverde de Lucerna thought Don Manuel a saint. He gave all his money, invited the poor into his home, spoke eloquently, and reached across the masses of his congregation to heal a wounded life. But if he ever tried to move a mountain with his faith, it would have crumbled to the sea. Where did the fault lie? If you asked Brown or Unamuno, the fault would lie with us, because we refuse to accept a postmodern view of relative truth.

But, again, what about this claim: "You will know the truth, and the truth will set you free" (John 8:32)? This language is not only profound, it is also ridiculously simple. The structure of the book of John was to simply say, "Here is the truth," and "Here is *why* it is the truth." B. F. Westcott said that it is characteristic of Christianity that it claims to be the Truth, when in reality it is Christ Himself who is the Truth.[9] Jesus is the one who claimed, "I am the truth." The truth is not *of* Jesus, but Jesus himself—his personality, his power, his presence. His very essence is *truth.*

Quid est veritas? We all ask it in one language or another, at one point or another in our life. Truth is always there in the voice that says to us, "This is the way; walk in it" (Isa. 30:21). What is truth? We *must* answer the question for ourselves and for the people who are going to ask us. How we do will determine the future of our society. Pilate, after asking it, ignored the Truth, Jesus himself, standing right in front of him, washed his hands, and walked away. What will *we* do?

Chapter 5

DON'T KNOW MUCH ABOUT HISTORY

Rumor has it Dan Brown is suffering from writer's block. We had hoped to have his new book, *The Solomon Key*, in hand by now to include in our analysis. We have a theory that Robert Langdon is actually Dan Brown, to some extent, and were interested in seeing what developments occur in Langdon's spiritual journey. But his new book isn't out yet. It was supposed to be released around the summer of 2005. Then it was going to be out "any day." Now, as we understand it, there is no release date scheduled because the book is nowhere near finished.

The *New York Times* is speculating why Brown hasn't released anything new in several years. One theory has it that he is concerned that anything he writes after *The Da Vinci Code* might be considered something of a letdown, so he might be experiencing performance anxiety.

But another theory the *Times* postulates is even more interesting. Could it be that Dan Brown is being more careful about his research now that so many folks have taken him to task for his historical blunders? He seemed so sure of himself and his research—almost challenging people to poke holes in it. And poke we did. We're not the only ones to point these things out. As previously mentioned, a slew of books has been released in the last two years, showing the historical errors for what they are: historical errors.

There is the claim that the Emperor Constantine moved the Christian day of worship from Saturday to Sunday. We know from the apostle Paul and other New Testament writers that shortly after the resurrection of Jesus, Christians began meeting together on the first day of the week to celebrate the resurrection and commemorate it by partaking of the Lord's Supper. They would encourage one another and remember what Jesus had done on their behalf, often singing hymns and having someone teach a lesson from Scripture. What Constantine did in AD 321 was to declare Sunday to be a day of rest from work. He did not make Sunday the day of worship for Christians; it was *already* that from the first century.

Brown also accuses Constantine of pressuring the bishops at the Council of Nicaea in 325 to vote to "make" Jesus divine: "Until *that* moment in his history Jesus was viewed by his followers as a mortal prophet, a great and powerful man, but a man nonetheless" (*DVC*, 233). We'll deal with this in more detail later, but, in the meantime, we join with Gerald O'Collins, Roman Catholic professor of theology at the Pontifical Gregorian University in Rome, who wishes someone would get Brown a copy of the Gospel of John and watch him read the part where it quotes Thomas saying, "My Lord and my God!" to the resurrected Jesus. Clearly, the deity of Jesus is affirmed in those pages. O'Collins asserts that "decades before John's Gospel was finished, St. Paul's letters repeatedly affirm faith in Christ as divine."[1] Jesus Christ was divine; the apostles believed it. The Council of Nicaea in 325 did not bestow divinity upon Christ; it merely reaffirmed what Christians had believed for centuries.

Some of Brown's fabrications really do appear to be just cheap attempts to titillate. The misinformation that Brown introduces regarding ritualistic sex in the temple at Jerusalem is one of his most egregious errors. Israelite men never came to the temple for a spiritual encounter by having sacred sex with priestesses. This was a real practice, but not a practice of Hebrews in the temple. This practice belonged in the temples of Athena or Aphrodite. Pagan sex rituals such as those engaged in during the worship of Baal or Molech (which also often involved child sacrifice) were consistently condemned by the Hebrew prophets. There were no priestesses offering sacred sex in the Jerusalem temple. There were no priestesses in the temple, period.

Continuing his case for the "divine feminine" and goddess worship, Brown, ignoring the Jewish roots of Christianity, again turns to pagan sources. He assures us that "virtually all the elements of Catholic ritual" were adapted directly from earlier pagan religions, ignoring, for example, the use of altars as explained in Leviticus. Brown likewise overlooks how communion had its origins in the Passover Feast, celebrated by Jesus and his disciples on the night he was betrayed.

Brown continues to demonstrate his misguided understanding of theological issues when he asserts that God and "his powerful female consort, Shekinah" shacked up in the Holy of Holies (that is, the innermost room of the temple in Jerusalem). The word *Shekinah* isn't even found in the Bible. Rather, this word, which refers to the closeness of God to his people and the beauty and weight of his presence, comes from later rabbinic literature. It has *nothing* to do with a female partner. It is also total nonsense to assert that the sacred name *YHWH* was derived from the ancient name *Jehovah* and relates to the word *Eve* ("Havah"). Eve has nothing to do with this name for God, and the word Jehovah is actually a derivative mispronunciation of Yahweh from the sixteenth century (hardly ancient). First came Yahweh, then Jehovah, not vice versa.

Need more to convince you that Brown didn't do enough homework? The Priory of Sion is vital to the plot of *The Da Vinci Code* and to the new religion Dan Brown is creating for us, as it is the secret keeper of information about Jesus' "true" story. But the ancient Priory of Sion is actually a relatively recent creation, a hoax based on a series of forgeries committed in the 1960s and 70s by a French con man, named Pierre Plantard, who later spent time in prison and died in 2000. When the book *Holy Blood, Holy Grail,* one of Brown's primary sources and one of the books Sophie finds in Teabing's study, was published in 1982, the three authors accepted the forged documents as genuine. A few years later, though, a series of books and a BBC documentary exposed the fraud, and the authors began to claim that they had been tricked by Plantard. Dan Brown's meticulous research should have turned up the details about all this;

about fifteen minutes on the Internet would have done the job. Perhaps it suits his purposes to keep the truth to himself.

We could spend an entire book picking out individual errors in Dan Brown's books, but others have done that already. Instead we're going to focus on two overarching themes Dan Brown consistently gets wrong: that Christianity is misogynistic and that it is diametrically opposed to science. After that, we will discuss why history doesn't mean the same thing to Dan Brown that it means to us.

Women and Christianization

"This novel is very empowering to women. Can you comment?" This question is posted on Brown's Web site. He responds: "2000 [*sic*] years ago, we lived in a world of gods and goddesses. Today, we live in a world solely of gods. Women, in most cultures, have been stripped of their spiritual power. The novel touches on the questions of how and why this shift occurred and on what lessons we might learn from it regarding our future."

Has the Christian church suppressed the "sacred feminine?" Admittedly, there has been far too much talk about the "submission of women in the church"—so much that we have sometimes forgotten about the subject of submission in general.

But Dan Brown claims that Christianity is based on misogyny and is inherently opposed to women's rights. People believe him because many who champion women's rights demonstrate open hostility toward traditional expressions of Christianity. Sadly, Christians *have* played a part in the subjugation of women in the past. But we cannot ignore the societal improvements regarding the role and status of women that have occurred *precisely because* of Christianity's influence.

In pre-Christian societies (those that existed before the arrival of Jesus and societies where Christianity has *never* been a dominant force) women were not revered as Dan Brown says. They were abused and oppressed. The worst abuses in the world are *still* being committed in nations where Christianity is violently opposed.

Here is a list of some practices of pre-Christian societies. Many of these actions were (or are) so common that they have names. One is the custom in ancient Greece of confining women to their quarters when men were present (*gynaeceum*). Another is the Roman Empire tradition of men holding such a degree of authority in their homes that they could sell their own daughters (*patria potestas*). Other forms of misogyny were infanticide and the Chinese custom of binding the feet of young girls to make them more attractive to Chinese men. Even today some African countries (and even some immigrants to our own country) are still practicing female castration (*clitoredectomy*).[2]

These practices seem horrific to our Christian-cultured minds. But it is Christianity that brought a stop to most of them. Sociology professor Alvin Schmidt writes that "before Christianity arrived, century upon century had brought little or no freedom or dignity to women in any pagan culture. In short, where else do women have more freedom, opportunity and human worth than in countries that have been highly influenced by the Christian ethic?"[3]

Christians are responsible for the outlawing of child abandonment and infanticide (not to mention the rescue and adoption of these children prior to these practices being abolished), an end to gladiatorial games (murder for sport), the opening of schools for poor children, the crusade for better treatment of the mentally ill, the idea of inalienable rights, and the origin of hospitals, schools, and elderly care facilities all over the United States. The history of Christianity has generally been one of advancement (with, granted, its moments of serious error). On balance, Christianity has advanced the cause for knowledge and civil rights for all people (including women).

Superstition and Scientific Progress

One theme dominates Brown's *Angels and Demons*: Christianity and science are in total opposition to each other. In *Angels and Demons*, the church perceives that science will kill it, so the church kills in order to stop science (sorry to spoil the story). In defense of his actions, the church leader who organizes the killings protests, "Science, you say, will save us. Science, I say, has destroyed us. Since the days of Galileo, the church has tried to slow the relentless march of science."

Seeing Christianity as the thwarter of science is a very popular fallacy. Since Andrew Dickson White wrote his book, *A History of the Warfare of Science with Theology in Christendom* in 1896, the idea has been accepted almost unquestioningly. However, the truth is exactly the opposite. As Walker Percy says in *Lost in the Cosmos*, "It is no coincidence that science sprang, not from Ionian metaphysics, not from the Brahmin-Buddhist-Taoist East, not from the Egyptian-Mayan astrological South, but from the heart of the Christian West, that although Galileo fell out with the church, he would hardly have taken so much trouble studying Jupiter and dropping objects from towers if the reality and value and order of things had not first been conferred by belief in the Incarnation."[4]

Historian of science Reijer Hooykaas determined that "most scientists of the nineteenth and twentieth centuries . . . have been unconscious of the fact that the metaphysical foundations of their discipline stemmed, in spite of all secularization, in great part from the biblical concept of God and creation."[5]

In his book, *How Christianity Changed the World*, Schmidt makes a well-documented case that Christianity, rather than being a force that has continuously opposed science, actually laid the foundations for modern science: "Ever since [White's book], along with the growth of secularism, countless professors have uncritically accepted White's argument that Christianity is an enemy of science, so it seems unthinkable to many that it could possibly have fostered the arrival of science. Given this widespread bias, the old adage comes to mind: 'A little knowledge is a dangerous thing'" (218–19).

Let's examine history to see if there's any positive connection between science and men of faith. Consider these examples: Jean Buridan (fourteenth century) introduced the theory of probability. Nicolaus Copernicus (fifteenth and sixteenth centuries) proposed the idea that the earth revolved around the sun (rather than the earth being the center of all things). Andreas Vesalius (sixteenth century) became the father of human anatomy. Galileo Galilei (sixteenth and seventeenth centuries) was the first person to use the telescope to study the skies. William Harvey (sixteenth century) discovered how blood circulated. Blaise Pascal (seventeenth century) built the first mechanical adding machine. Sir Isaac Newton (eighteenth century) identified the law of gravity. Joseph Priestly (eighteenth century) isolated and described the properties of oxygen, carbon dioxide, and nitrous oxide (and discovered soda pop). Michael Faraday (nineteenth century) discovered the principle of electromagnetism. Louis Pasteur (nineteenth century) founded the science of microbiology and created the first vaccines. Gregor Mendel (nineteenth century) laid the foundation for modern genetics. Obstetrician James Simpson (nineteenth century) laid the foundations for modern anesthesia (especially in childbirth—another boon to women). Joseph Lister (nineteenth and twentieth centuries) introduced antiseptics into the operating room.[6]

All of these men were Christians; many were even sponsored by the church. Moreover, they did not engage in scientific discovery *in spite* of their religious beliefs. Rather, they engaged in scientific discovery *because* of their religious beliefs. They understood nature as part of God's creation, designed to bring him glory, and they knew that God had commissioned them as stewards of this creation. And they believed they should work toward a greater understanding of how things work.

Physics professor Stanley Jaki, author of *Savior of Science,* suggests that science suffered "still births" in other civilizations. Because of the religious presuppositions of the Egyptians, Babylonians, and even the Greeks, scientific study could not develop fully within those societies. And from the time of Aristotle until the arrival of brave Christian scientists like Roger Bacon, William Occam, and Francis Bacon, the entire scientific world generally held to the Aristotelian theory that knowledge could only be acquired "through the deductive processes of the mind." In short, this meant that knowledge could only be discovered by *thinking* and not by *doing.* Inductive method, "which required manual activity, was taboo. Physical activities were only for slaves, not for thinkers or freemen." Had such scientists as Occam, the Bacons, Buridan, Vesalius, Galileo, and others not seen God and nature as distinct, had they been pantheists like the scientists before them, there would be no science as we understand it today.[7]

Unfortunately, about 100 years ago someone told us that science had nothing to do with religion, and many of us believed him. Therefore, Christian foundations for science are generally not taught in schools, be they elementary or university. As Schmidt relates:

> [T]his great omission became institutionalized, and thus today's students—and the public—are unaware that virtually all scientists from the Middle Ages to the mid-eighteenth century—many of whom were seminal thinkers—not only were sincere Christians but were often inspired by biblical postulates and premises in their theories that sought to explain and predict natural phenomena. These pioneering scientists, upon whose shoulders present-day scientists stand, knew and believed the words of the biblical writer: "The heavens declare the glory of God; the skies proclaim the work of his hands" (Psalm 19:1). To them, God could not be factored out. And concerning their Christian faith, they echoed the words of [Johannes] Kepler: "I am in earnest about Faith, and I do not play with it." They were 180 degrees removed from the relativistic cliché of today's post-modernism that says, "What is true for you is not true for me." To them, truth was one, and God was its Author. (244)

You can sum it all up this way: Christianity is historically pro-woman and pro-science, but you'd never know that from reading any of Dan Brown's books. And there's a reason for that: Dan Brown doesn't really believe in history.

Revising Dan Brown

In the movie *The Princess Bride*, the character Vizzini keeps using the word *inconceivable*. The joke is that every time he says something is inconceivable, it turns out to be true. Eventually, another character innocently says, "You keep using that word. I do not think it means what you think it means." That's the problem with Dan Brown's research. He keeps using the word *history*, but we do not think it means what he thinks it means.

He isn't really that interested in historic events as they actually happened. He's more interested in telling you *his version* of those events (the very same thing, by the way, that he accuses "the church" of doing). So the question is, What is history?

History: The Way We Imagine We Were

Relativism has made significant inroads in the field of historical knowledge. History used to be defined as "that which has happened as well as the record of it."[7] In other words, history was a study of the past—the search for knowledge of what actually took place in the past. In fact, the word *history* comes from the Greek root word *historeo,* meaning "research"—"it implies the act of judging the evidences in order to separate fact from fiction. . . . Originally, research set the historian apart from the poet and the maker of myths or legends. They told stories, too; but only the historian restricted himself to telling a story based on the facts ascertained by inquiry of research."[8]

The assumption used to be that certain events took place at certain times for certain reasons. We believed that we could find out about those events and understand how and why they happened as long as the effects of those events still survived and could be found. We also believed that the more accurate our understanding of the past, the more effectively we could act in the present and plan for the future.

This philosophy of history is now widely regarded as obsolete and irrelevant. We are now told that history is constructed according to the perspectives (i.e., biases) of the historian and that there is no objective way to judge which perspectives must be used and no way to be sure that our constructions correspond to the way things "really" were. In other words, as Sir Leigh Teabing says, "History is always written by the winners. When two cultures clash, the loser is obliterated, and the winner writes the history books—books [that] glorify their own cause and disparage the conquered foe. As Napoleon once said, 'What is history but a fable agreed upon?'" (*DVC,* 256).

Teabing, Brown's character, is speaking for Brown himself. Note the correlation of Teabing's quote with one from Brown: "It's interesting to note . . . that since the beginning of recorded time, history has been written by the 'winners' (those societies and belief systems that conquered and survived). Many historians now believe (as do I) that in gauging the historical accuracy of a given concept, we should first ask ourselves a far deeper question: How historically accurate is history itself?"[9]

So history itself is not historically accurate, but the things presented in his books are "historical fact"? Hmm, that's a problem. On page 256, the expert Teabing says that history is written by the winners and shouldn't really be trusted. But eleven pages earlier, Teabing claims that "the marriage of Jesus and Mary Magdalene is part of the historical record." What historical record? The one that can't be trusted? Interesting.

As we're about to see, postmodernists keep using the word *history,* but they don't think it means what we think it means.

No one doubts that historians are guided by their own assumptions, experiences, training, and values, and that these factors play a part in shaping the conclusions they reach. But it doesn't follow that these subjective factors render historians incapable of recording objective facts. Still, the idea that history is all a matter of perspective and that historicity is in the eye of the beholder is the prevailing attitude in some academic circles.

Many postmodern historians are quite open about the fact that, in their view, history serves ideological purposes. That is, the purpose of history is not to learn what actually happened in the past (which is supposedly an impossible goal), but rather to further a social or political agenda. Usually, that agenda is one of liberating oppressed peoples and providing a voice for those whose perspective has been ignored or suppressed by the powerful. This is a noble goal but one that is well beyond the scope of the study of history.

This ideological philosophy of history is self-defeating, as one can only serve the interests of the oppressed peoples if it is possible to identify who the oppressed peoples actually are. Every citation of slavery, genocide, persecution, or marginalization of a people group assumes that we can examine the facts and agree that *in fact* the people in question did receive such treatment.

Afrocentrism: Teaching Myth as History

An excellent example of this trend is Afrocentrism, an attempt to claim African origins for numerous famous people, inventions, and cultural developments traditionally attributed to European or other non-African sources. Searching for the actual contributions of African peoples to the history and cultures of the world and exposing how some African contributions have been overlooked is a worthwhile scholarly pursuit. But Afrocentrism is troubling in its disregard for the facts and its open encouragement, at least on the part of some, to see history as a tool for proving a point rather than a pursuit of the truth.

Mary Lefkowitz has authored an insightful critique of Afrocentric revisionism in her book *Not Out of Africa*, in which she refutes the claim that Socrates was black and that the Greeks stole their philosophy and other intellectual legacies from African culture. Lefkowitz, a Jewish historian, is understandably sensitive to people revising history to suit their political agendas, since the Nazis created fictions about Jewish history to justify the Holocaust, and since more than a half century later a stubborn minority of people in the West still deny that the Holocaust even happened.

Academics ought to have seen right from the start that this "new historicism" has some serious shortcomings. But in fact most of us are just beginning to emerge from the fog far enough to see where history-without-facts can lead us, which is right back to fictive history of the kind developed to serve the Third Reich. It is not coincidental that ours is the era not just of Holocaust denial but of denial that the ancient Greeks were ancient Greeks and creators of their own intellectual heritage. . . . There are of course many possible interpretations of the truth, but some things are simply not true. It is not true that there was no Holocaust. There was a Holocaust, although we may disagree about the numbers of people killed. Likewise, it is not true that the Greeks stole their philosophy from Egypt."[10]

Any attempt to evade this problem by claiming that there are different "truths" and that the Afrocentrists are as entitled to their truth as anyone else misses the point. Postmodern historians are not seeking tolerance; they are demanding (and, in some cases, getting) official endorsement as the new historical paradigm in universities and throughout the educational establishment. Competition among conflicting theories or beliefs is nothing new in academia; what is new is basing the studies not on facts but preferences. Lefkowitz asks, "Are there, can there be, multiple, diverse 'truths'? If there are, which 'truth' should win? The one that is most loudly argued, or most persuasively phrased? Diverse 'truths' are possible only if 'truth' is understood to mean something like 'point of view.' The notion of diversity does not extend to truth" (162).

Among other numerous examples of relativistic history, consider the debates about the place of Christopher Columbus in history that raged during 1992 or the revisionist history offered by Oliver Stone in such movies as *JFK*—these and many more have paved the way for Dan Brown's revision of church history, the Bible, and western civilization.

Recovering a Christian View of History

Back in school, history required long hours spent learning dates and names and places. And if you wanted to pass an exam covering, say, the Industrial Revolution, you had to be able to give the dates of the Industrial Revolution. But you rarely, if ever, had to tell why the Industrial Revolution happened or why it's important to know about it.

History doesn't give us a good reason up front for studying it. We know it's important to speak and read and write well—that's why we study English. We know it's important to balance a checkbook or figure out how to carpet the downstairs of our home—that's why we study math and geometry. One trip to the doctor's office, and you'll be glad you paid attention in your science class. But history? What is it good for?

And then there's the way history is presented in most schools. History is packed with kid-engaging delights: battles and spies, distant lands and heroes. You'd think we would all love history class. But the truth is (and studies have shown this) most of us hated history class. We love history, but we loathe the way we're expected to learn it. Could that be by design?

We think it might be.[11]

Most of what children learn in school is colored by a particular philosophy: the philosophy of evolution. Evolution tells us that life happened accidentally. There was no intention, no design, no purpose. It follows, then, that everything is random. Nothing happens for any kind of reason. It's just a bunch of arbitrary events. And details don't matter if it's all one pointless accident.

Evolution also tells us that new is better than old. Old is archaic. New is improved. We are enlightened. Back in the olden days, people were superstitious and needed to believe in God to protect them from the boogeyman. We can't learn anything from people in the past. It would be like asking a four-year-old to help you with your marriage.

If evolution provides the lens through which we view all academic pursuits, then studying history is kind of silly. What happened in the past doesn't have any real impact on us today. But if evolution is wrong, then history matters.

We believe God created the world and runs it. History is part of his creation, and, like the rest of creation, is designed to bring him honor and glory. Before God created history, he determined how he wanted it to end. It will be this climactic act—the one toward which history is inevitably moving—that will infuse every minute of human history, every detail with meaning and purpose. God created history for a reason, and when that reason is fulfilled, history will cease to exist. We'll all move into a realm known as eternity. If we understand this, we will better understand history.

History is largely shaped by a conflict between two spiritual kingdoms that are vying for control of humanity. The Bible tells us that there is an enemy of God, and he is known by many names: Satan, Lucifer, the Devil. The Bible also tells us that this enemy of God has his own kingdom (Matt. 12:26), devoted to spreading evil throughout the earth (2 Cor. 4:4). The Bible tells us clearly that the outcome of this conflict has already been decided, but that hasn't stopped the enemy from fighting. Instead, he seems to be walking wounded (much like the Louvre curator at the beginning of *The Da Vinci Code*).

Your perspective on history is important. If history really is a reflection of a cosmic battle (that involved holocausts and happier times), wouldn't this explain a lot about why history is filled with grace and beauty while being littered with tragedy and misery at the same time?

What if history isn't just random events strung loosely together by war winners but is instead a grand stage upon which the most thrilling drama of all times is unfolding? If history is designed to bring glory and honor to God, then God's character and nature should be revealed in the sweep of history.

Karl Marx once said, "A people without a heritage are easily persuaded." Stephen Mansfield says, "But a people who have a heritage, particularly a godly heritage, have a strong sense of where they are going—in part because they recognize the flow of history [that] gives meaning and a sense of importance to their existence. . . . This is one of the greatest blessings of history. To know how others have 'fought the good fight' will light a fire of inspiration in our own lives."[11]

History matters.

Chapter 6

NO DOUBLE STANDARDS ALLOWED

"I don't know how to love him."
— Andrew Lloyd Webber, *Jesus Christ Superstar*

Shirley sat cross-legged in her backyard, praying. She didn't know why; she had never prayed before. It was 1974, and Shirley had gone with several of her friends to see the popular rock opera, *Jesus Christ Superstar*. Even though she had grown up in a relatively conservative part of Missouri, this was the first time Shirley had ever heard any form of the gospel story. And it moved her.

Through all the musical spectacle, athletic choreography, and angst-ridden lyrics, the story itself had an unmistakable power that shone through. Shirley found herself remembering a portion of the lyrics as she stared at her back fence, and before she realized it, tears began to leak down her face. She knew, somehow, that Jesus was real. She knew that he was more than she had ever reckoned and that he was reaching out to her. The lyrics to Mary Magdalene's song reverberated in her head: "I don't know how to love him." *That's what I want*, she thought. *I want to know how to love him*. That became her prayer that day, and it continues to be her prayer to this day.

Shirley is not the only one who has been introduced to the gospel message through an avenue other than the Bible or an official church-related activity. Many people first hear about Jesus through songs, films, television shows, and conversations and embark on a search for more.

Shirley didn't assume that Andrew Lloyd Webber and Tim Rice were divinely inspired. She knew the musical was popular, but she didn't go around quoting the lyrics as if they were Scripture. Instead, she went to the Bible and sought people who were authentically living out their relationship with Jesus. They pointed her to some authors— C. S. Lewis and G. K. Chesterton and Augustine. These great thinkers laid out their arguments for why Christianity makes sense to them and why Christianity can withstand scrupulous investigation.

Shirley didn't take anyone's word for anything but looked into matters for herself and came away with a deep appreciation for what Christianity is. In the end she made a leap of faith, but it was no leap into the dark; it was a leap into the light.

Dan Brown suggests that orthodox Christians who believe in things like the Bible, the virgin birth, and the deity of Christ are naive and ignorant. One of his characters in *Angels and Demons* says that people simply believe what they are raised to believe, thus asserting that most Christians believe what they're told without asking any questions or doing any research. Shirley would be offended at those accusations, because that wasn't what she did at all. Admittedly, many Christians have failed to love God with their minds and rigorously engage in intellectual pursuits. And some *have* accepted what is handed to them without a morsel of personal scholarship. But there are many, many others for whom this has not been the case.

We won't take the time here to provide any kind of exhaustive bibliography, but we are indebted to thinkers and philosophers like C. S. Lewis, G. K. Chesterton, and Augustine. We also heartily recommend books by Lee Strobel, Norm Geisler, Josh McDowell, and Ravi Zacharias. Our point here, however, is that Christians need to think about matters of faith and scholarship. And we applaud those who, like the writers we've just mentioned, do just that.

But let's turn the tables a little and ask another probing question: Just how meticulous has Dan Brown been in his research? Could Mr. Brown be guilty of doing the same thing he accuses Christians of doing? Could it be that he has simply accepted the opinions of others without searching out truth on his own?

Mediocrity Makes the Media

The media, in all their Hollywood brilliance, has praised Dan Brown's research as impeccable. Take the review from bookreporter .com: "Dan Brown's extensive research on secret societies and symbology adds intellectual depth to this page-turning thriller. His surprising revelations on da Vinci's penchant for hiding codes in his paintings will lead the reader to search out renowned artistic icons . . . you will never see [these] famous painting[s] in quite the same way again."

You've heard us say this before, but here we go again: Brown's research is heavily flawed. Authors' note to readers: We have poured through books, articles, and personal correspondence with experts in various fields to bring you this fact-based summary of the research snags in Brown's book, but do your own research so that you don't also become guilty of Mr. Brown's indictments upon Christian thinkers. There is joy to be found in loving God with your mind. We would love it if you would do the research on your own and correct us if we need it. For now, we'll start by looking at Dan Brown the art critic.

Amateur Art Critique

The Last Supper, which is located in the refectory (i.e., eating area for the monks) of Santa Maria delle Grazie church in Milan, Italy, forms the artistic centerpiece of *The Da Vinci Code*. In his painting, Leonardo purposefully groups the disciples in trios, isolating Jesus at the center of the scene and playing the disciples' reactions off of one another. In this careful composition, Leonardo's four groups of three apostles attain a very precise and formal symmetry. The result is a dazzling juxtaposition of figures and sharply contrasting attitudes, in which Judas guiltily withdraws from Christ while Peter vigorously addresses his request to an impressionable and attentive John.

The artist intentionally uses a V-shaped space to separate the two groups of figures in *The Last Supper* for artistic balance. Brown, however, ignores this Renaissance painting technique and instead makes the outrageous claim that this V-shaped space is one of many visual clues painted by Leonardo to symbolically represent the chalice, or the sacred feminine. Real art critics will tell you that the space between the two figures actually expresses the concept of *dynamic masses* found in Renaissance art. Apparently, codes are in the eye of the beholder.

Brown's Sir Leigh Teabing says, "Oddly, Da Vinci appears to have forgotten to paint the cup of Christ" (*DVC*, 236)—as if Leonardo, living 1,500 years after the actual event, conclusively, exhaustively, and accurately portrayed all the nuances of an event he had only read about. Further, the central issue emphasized in the painting was not Jesus' sacrifice; it was Judas' betrayal of Jesus. This painting specifically dramatizes the moment when Jesus warns, "One of you will betray me." Leonardo's composition conforms to traditional Florentine depictions of the Last Supper, stressing the betrayal and sacrifice of Jesus, rather than the institution of the Eucharist and the chalice.

Langdon also finds it significant that Jesus and the figure seated on His right form the letter *M,* supposedly signifying that Mary Magdalene is beside him. The novel states: "Sophie saw it at once. To say the letter leapt out at her was an understatement. . . . Glaring in the center of the painting was the unquestionable outline of an enormous, flawlessly performed letter M" (*DVC*, 245). You can see by looking at the painting yourself that this is far from a perfect letter *M.* In fact, the only way you can get an *M* out of it is

to include the whole triad, including Peter and Judas, which would defeat the whole point about this referring to Mary Magdalene. But you can find all sorts of "hidden letter codes" in the painting if you try. Maybe it's actually a *V* for "Vinci"? Or an upside-down *W* for "Who made this up?"

We should also note that the Renaissance tradition followed by Leonardo was that of painting young men with a measure of effeminateness to express the androgynous appearance of youth. Incidentally, a painting of John the Baptist hangs in the Louvre next to *The Madonna of the Rocks*, another key painting in Brown's novel. In

that painting, John the Baptist looks more than a little like a woman to us. There are many, many paintings in this period where young men look significantly feminine.

Let's look back to John's Gospel for the account of the Last Supper: "After he had said this, Jesus was troubled in spirit and testified, 'I tell you the truth, one of you is going to betray me.' His disciples stared at one another, at a loss to know which of them he meant. One of them, the disciple whom Jesus loved, was reclining next to him. Simon Peter motioned to this disciple and said, 'Ask him which one he means.' Leaning back against Jesus, he asked him, 'Lord, who is it?'" (13:21–25).

This is the pregnant moment dramatically captured in *The Last Supper*. Notice from the masculine pronouns in this account that Peter gestures to a male, one of the disciples whom Jesus loved, and asked this male, John, to reveal the identity of the betrayer. If this beloved disciple is not John, but actually Mary Magdalene as the novel claims, this raises the obvious question that is overlooked in this book: Where was John—one of the three most prominent disciples, especially when the other eleven are all portrayed?

We mentioned this a few paragraphs ago, but we should really state it plainly. Leonardo da Vinci may, in fact, have drawn a woman into his famous "fresco," but he wasn't there at the actual event any more than we were. He drew really nice pictures and perhaps saw a means of goosing the church, which, God knows, can always use some goosing. More than likely, he was using a technique that was extremely common in his time (i.e., painting male youths as androgynous), but even if he wasn't, so what? Leonardo did not claim his picture was an accurate historical depiction of the event. Odds are, the disciples in that room didn't line up on one side of the table like they do in television sitcoms. Leonardo did not issue a disclaimer stating that everything in his paintings was based on factual research. The artist didn't make that mistake; Dan Brown did.

This lack of accurate interpretation of art runs rampant in Brown's work. He also calls *The Last Supper* a fresco, but it is not—and this is a significant discrepancy. If the painting had been a fresco—painted with egg tempera on *wet* plaster, as was the practice at the time—we would still have a first-class original painting to ponder instead of the heavily and repeatedly restored version Leonardo painted on *dry* plaster. It seems Leonardo wanted to play around with a new method he had invented so he could use more colors and redo portions if necessary. The painting took him four years to finish, angering his patrons because of the delay. Brown spends the majority of an entire chapter calling the painting a fresco when it clearly is not. This seems like nit-picking, but it raises a question: If Brown can't even get his art history right, why would someone buy his theology? Or, if the man spent years meticulously researching the material in this book but missed this obvious detail, what kind of scholarship was he reading? We'll talk about that in a minute, but first let's look at Dan Brown's pseudo-scholarly theological assertions.

Ersatz Education

Let's start by further exploring Brown's claim that the tetragrammaton *JHVH* derives from an androgynous physical union between the masculine (*Yah*) and the pre-Hebraic name for Eve (*Havah*). This is simply false, because we know that the word *Jehovah* is a sixteenth-century German rendering of *YHVH* that added the vowels of *Adonai*, a name which means "Lord," to the tetragrammaton *JHVH*. Thus, the consonants *Y-H-V-H* were combined with the vowels from Adonai (the *A-O-A* portion), producing *Yahovah,* which then became *Jehovah*. Brown's claim regarding this most holy Jewish name reflects a lack of basic understanding of this word's etymology.

We also find it interesting that Bruce Boucher, a curator at the Art Institute of Chicago, tags Brown's references to Leonardo da Vinci by saying they "show that his grasp of the historical Leonardo is shaky." Boucher explains that da Vinci is no surname but simply a reference to the fact that he was the illegitimate son of Ser Piero of Vinci.[1] Adding to the charm of *that* error, the claim that the name *Mona Lisa* is an anagram for the names of the Egyptian god Amon and the Egyptian goddess Isis is impossible, because of the extra "n" in the *proper* spelling of *Monna* (short for *Madonna*). Irresponsible, not impeccable, research.

Now, for our all-time favorite: In the last page of *The Da Vinci Code*, Langdon confirmed his hunches when he "emerged into a large chamber." This so-called chamber is supposed to be the location of the burial place of Mary Magdalene but is actually a shopping mall outside a lower entrance to the Louvre. (Not to mention that we wait the entire length of the book to find out the actual location of the Holy Grail, and it turns out the "actual place" doesn't exist.) If a reader has bought into *anything* in Brown's book, hopefully by this point he or she has clued in to why it's labeled as fiction. But if not, it might help to note that he doesn't put the "Grail" in a mysterious place. He tells us the precise location, and if you actually go there yourself you'll find—oh the irony—a Virgin Records store. Mary Magdelene's Mall, if you will.

So, at the end of the day, not only is Dan Brown promoting heresy, he's not all that good at doing it. A friend of ours said that she couldn't finish the book because the writing was so sloppy. If she had read on, she might have seen that it's not just his writing that is slapdash; he's not even careful with his *own* information. On page 220, Teabing's driveway is a mile long, and on page 279, it's only a half-mile. Also, current frequenters and patrons of the Louvre may balk at Brown's proposed distance traversed by a mortally wounded seventy-six-year-old man from the Grand Gallery to the curator's office, as it is—in reality—several city blocks in distance. As we have seen, his attempts at research are pitiful. Perhaps one reason his conclusions are so easy to debunk is because his sources are corrupt. Let's take a closer look at some of the books on Teabing's shelves.

Scandalous Sources

In the February 28, 2003 issue of Denver, Colorado's *Rocky Mountain News,* a reviewer claimed that *The Da Vinci Code* is a "rare book that manages to both entertain and educate simultaneously," adding that "there is enough medieval history to please any historian."

First of all, the ideas contained in *The Da Vinci Code* are far from rare, as its author's conjectures have been posed by a handful of so-called researchers in past years. The one factor that makes this book different is that it is wrapped up in a thrilling murder mystery. The mystery provides Brown a platform on which to feed his readers shoddy scholarship. Many of Brown's assertions are simply a regurgitation of conspiracy theories set forth by extremists and marginal scholars, not great historians.

As much as he may accuse Christians of being creations of their environment, Dan Brown is postmodernism's own creation. Postmodern scholarship says that you need only read the sources that agree with your hypothesis and demonize the ones that don't.

Unfortunately, this is the standard in many academic institutions today. We have a friend who attended a seminary where one of his professors told him, "I don't read evangelical scholars. Why should I? I already know what they're going to say." The reading list from his professor didn't require (or even encourage) students to read conservative scholars. This biased reading list thwarted the seminarian's education—he didn't know the basics; that's why he was taking the classes. As a result, his education came almost exclusively from fringe scholarship. That's an irresponsible professor practicing irresponsible scholarship in an irresponsible institution.

When students are only allowed to read certain sources that all tend to agree on everything, it is known as *closed scholarship*. Students should be exposed to good arguments from differing viewpoints and taught to recognize valid points where they exist. Christians should not fall prey to the idea that only those who agree with us are worthy of being heard.

Such closed scholarship is found in Dan Brown's research. Dan Brown has used five or six writers who are academically disreputable and quote only each other. But how is the average reader to know that he is simply looking to people who are all of the same opinion? Well, he discloses his sources, for the most part, by mentioning that the "renowned art historian" Sir Leigh Teabing keeps these great books in his library and uses them to enlighten people, like Sophie.

Poor Sophie.

Here are just a few of Brown's/Teabing's "sources" and some brief information concerning each of these so-called academics.

Holy Blood, Holy Grail

AUTHORS: Michael Baigent, Richard Leigh, and Henry Lincoln. By the way, if you look closely, you'll probably see where Dan Brown got the name for Sir Leigh Teabing (hint: ignore Lincoln and make your own anagram of *Baigent*).

THE BIG IDEA: Baigent, Leigh, and Lincoln present an argument in favor of a conspiratorial view of Western history. They suggest that Jesus may have survived the crucifixion and his wife, Mary Magdalene, traveled with their child (or children) to what is now France. There they established what became the Merovingian dynasty, which is now championed by the Priory of Sion, a secret society.

THE BIG PROBLEM: Two of these authors were Masonic historians and one is a writer of fiction. These authors are suing Brown's publisher for infringement of intellectual property, specifically for "lifting the whole architecture" of Brown's book from their 1982 "nonfiction" book.[2] Brown asserts that there are documents supporting the existence of the Priory of Sion in the Bibliotheque Nationale. These documents have long been understood to be forgeries, created and placed in the archives (designed to look old and just stuck behind some books) by an anti-Semitic supporter of the Vichy government named Pierre Plantard. He was called into court to testify in a semi-related matter in 1993 and, under oath, admitted that he had fabricated the whole thing.

The Goddess in the Gospels: Reclaiming the Sacred Feminine and Woman with the Alabaster Jar: Mary Magdalene and the Holy Grail

AUTHOR: Margaret Starbird

THE BIG IDEA: Starbird puts together a horde of ideas to "prove" that Jesus and Mary were married, had children, and moved to France. She also seems obsessed with telling people that the sun and the moon actually got together on a Pope's birthday in this century to try to tell him that the church has been "eclipsing" the sacred feminine.

THE BIG PROBLEM: Both of these books prove that if you decide the outcome before you start to do your research, the matter's already settled. Starbird has been studying this one thing for thirty years and appears extremely superstitious. She's not a respected scholar in any sense of either of those two words.

The Gnostic Gospels

AUTHOR: Elaine Pagels

THE BIG IDEA: Pagels defines a *gnostic* as "one who knows"—who by personal, experiential insight has attained a knowledge of God beyond that of the "common" Christian. She quotes the Gospel according to Philip: "Faith is our earth, in which we take root; hope is the water through which we are nourished; love is the air through which we grow; gnosis is the light through which we become fully grown." Sounds spiritual to me. Sounds fresh and bold to millions of others. So what's the problem?

THE BIG PROBLEM: The problem is we've checked all the Christian Bibles on our shelves and can't find the Gospel of Philip; it's not in there. And this is far from some kind of new-age stuff. Actually, this is quite old-age—1,850 years old. The Gnostic gospels were not suppressed by the apostles, as Pagels asserts, because they were not written while the apostles were alive. There's not a reputable scholar who will suggest that they were written before AD 150. There are some who might suggest that the Gospel of Thomas has an earlier date, but this is entirely based on the mythical scroll such scholars simply refer to as *Q*.

We want to say that again to make sure you understand: The only way the Gospel of Thomas is legitimately old enough to be valid is if there is this document called *Q*. No one has ever seen it. It does not exist. It was invented—guessed into existence—by people who were looking for a reason to undermine the authority of the four Gospels we have in the New Testament.

Elaine Pagels presents Gnosticism as an alternative version of early Christianity—the same story told from another side. According to her, these Gnostic "Christians" have been victims of a culture war waged by politically motivated and power-hungry bishops. According to actual scholarship, however, there is no evidence that there were two versions of Christianity that developed alongside each other. The first message was the message we have in the New Testament. Later—most scholars point to the second century AD—a heretical message developed: the Gnostic heresy.

The Templar Revelation: Secret Guardians of the True Identity of Christ

AUTHORS: Lynn Picknett and Clive Prince

THE BIG IDEA: Picknett and Prince retrace the ancestors and offspring of the Knights Templar, who were maliciously concealed early in the fourteenth century and investigate the nature of the secret knowledge they were said to have shared. They also trace the development of another secret society that arose alongside the Knights of Templar: the Priory of Sion. In the process, Picknett and Prince assert that everything you know about Christianity is wrong (sound familiar?). The Nativity is a myth, the life of Jesus has been misrepresented, and the Crucifixion was probably a publicity stunt gone bad. All proof of these accusations has been suppressed by men bent on promoting their own agenda, starting with Peter and Paul. Oh, these are the same authors who wrote a whole book claiming that the Shroud of Turin is actually a photograph of Leonardo da Vinci.

THE BIG PROBLEM: Where shall we start? The logic of Picknett and Prince is baffling. They seem to believe that whatever seems to have neither merit nor meaning must be both true and vitally important. With this upside-down viewpoint, the authors plunge into an investigation of the world of heresy and occultism. As one reviewer for CNN says, "Nothing in *The Templar Revelation* rises to anything like the level of 'definite proof.' Instead, its conclusions are based on the flimsiest of premises which are supported by the slimmest of indirect and circumstantial evidence or, just as often, by the assertion that the lack of evidence justifies their conclusions."[3]

Those books are what Dan Brown thinks of as scholarly research.

Sir Leigh Teabing's library is filled with these kind of obscure, pseudo-intellectual writings. These unreliable sources reveal the lack of careful scholarship that's required for a novel that claims to contain valid and accurate historical, architectural, aesthetic, and mathematical facts. All of the above are radical fringe "scholars" with the exception of Pagels, who is a bit closer to mainline liberalism. Still, all display a radical agenda of iconoclastic overthrow of traditional authority, morality, and ethos and lack an unbiased commitment to true scholarship.

In a tirade of moral indignation, Teabing says, "Shall the world be ignorant forever? Shall the church be allowed to cement its lies into our history books for all eternity? Shall the church be permitted to influence, indefinitely with murder and extortion? No. Something needs to be done" (*DVC*, 408–409). Thus, Brown accuses the church multiple times of demonizing certain good things and then recasting them as something totally opposite. Yet, most readers of *The Da Vinci Code* fail to notice that he offers no evidence to support these allegations. See any endnotes in any of Dan Brown's books? Nope, because his "research" did not have to pass the muster of peer review. It could not have.

Brown, through Teabing, makes a number of false, ham-fisted claims—all the while giving them an air of scholarship by having a scholar say them.

Circular Research

"Dan Brown has to be one of the best, smartest, and most accomplished writers in the country. *The Da Vinci Code* . . . is pure genius," says Nelson Demille.

While that is a nice quote to have on the back of your book, this "smart" book makes indiscriminate but very convincing claims concerning anti-Christian philosophies and agenda, yet offers no hint as to whether these are viable theories nor who initially discovered them. Brown's characters decide that the historic church has really "made up" their foundational teachings, which are merely ineffective attempts at solving the world's problems, and thus declare that this new solution succeeds where the others fail. The book may be ingenious, but only in that its author knew how to write a suspense story that would make the average reader ignore its many flaws.

It should be aggravating to the reader that he or she has no easy way of impartially criticizing Brown's positions without being viewed as closed-minded or duped. However, if one is knowledgeable about the information discussed in Dan Brown's books, it will help the reader to define the inherent problems of Brown's fabricated solution. If there is no attempt at some semblance of scholarship, the reader remains clueless and willing to say, "Hey, wow, that really makes you think!"

But if read as is, Brown's writings really make you *not* think and therein lies the problem. Dan Brown's book is rare in that it actually makes you more ignorant of history after you've read it than you were before.

Shirley's Jesus and How to Love Him

Many people are searching for answers in this world. Every human being on this planet will search for meaning. There are many Shirleys in this world who sit in their backyards of belief and ponder if there really is something to Jesus—or to Buddha—or to Mona Lisa's smile. Many turn to a religion for the answers, for religion explains the nature of the divine and how humans can come to terms with it. Shirley turned to personal scholarship and then to Jesus.

But there is a certain uniform deliverance in which religions all appear to meet. According to William James, this common element has two parts: an *uneasiness* (a sense that there is something wrong with us as we naturally stand) and a *solution* (how to fix it). It is "a sense that we are saved from the wrongness by making proper connection with the higher powers."[4] Sensing (and perhaps feeling himself) this postmodern uneasiness with traditional authority, morality, and ethos, Dan Brown has offered his own solution. In this sense, he has created his own religion.

This is the reason we do not see this book as merely fiction, but as agenda. There are far too many people who will accept its message in their own search for meaning. And his is not a religion based on truth, authority, or even good research, but in deception, conspiracy, and poor investigation. No one wants to base their convictions on that kind of nonsense. The stakes are too high.

It is our prayer that our readers, Christian or not, will consider themselves amateur scholars. One does not have to have a degree in theology or symbology or world religion to intelligibly search for truth. Real truth-seekers who believe in things like the Bible, the virgin birth, and the deity of Christ are not so naive and ignorant when they've spent time investigating the truth-claims of the world's religions. Please don't let someone else think for you; don't do what you're told without asking any questions or doing any research. Go to reliable sources, to people who live authentically, and at times, to your own gut. Search in earnest and you will find what you're looking for. After all, Jesus himself said that everyone who seeks will find.

Chapter 7

THANKING
DAN BROWN

"This [novel] is not a threat. This is an opportunity.
We are called to creatively engage the culture, and this is
what I want to do. I think Dan Brown has done me a favor.
He's letting me talk about things that matter."

— Father John Sewell, St. John's Episcopal Church
in Memphis, Tennessee

*I*n an attempt to be gracious, some Christian leaders have failed
to draw appropriate boundaries. Father John Sewell isn't the only
one thanking Dan Brown for giving the Christian community an
occasion to dialogue. Many have taken Mr. Brown at his word when
he said he just wanted us to all come together and have passionate
discussions about religion. These people probably really believe that,
instead of doing harm to our faith, Brown has actually handed us
an opportunity.

We respectfully disagree. Sure, talk about the concepts presented
in Brown's books abounds; but is it actually doing any good for the
cause of Christ? At another time in America's history, maybe fifty or
sixty years ago, discussions of this nature might have actually been
beneficial. At that time, people had greater knowledge of history, a
better understanding of the nature of truth, and a greater respect
for the Bible.

Introducing these ideas into a society where many are biblically
illiterate and prefer *seeking* truth to *finding* it (whatever "truth" may

mean to that individual) does not produce greater enlightenment; it produces more confusion. In this culture of relativism, discussing incorrect assumptions about religion may be more damaging than not discussing religion at all. Dan Brown's books have compounded the problems already brewing in pluralistic, postmodern society, creating a recipe for philosophical disaster.

Muddy Waters

Dan Brown has not done the Christian community a favor; he has simply muddied the waters, making it more difficult than ever to communicate the truth without having your motives called into question. Conveniently, Dan Brown can respond to anyone who calls his research into question by saying, "You simply believe what you were taught to believe. Therefore, you are proving my point."

It is difficult to engage in a cogent dialogue because Dan Brown has taken words and ideas that were, at one time, easily understood by all and given them new definitions. History, for example, is no longer a record of actual events that took place in time and space. History is now a distorted version of events that may or may not have taken place, designed to make the winner of the era or events look good.

Truth is no longer something that is revealed and discovered; truth is something that is created by individuals as we each carve out our own paths in this world. God does not ask us all to live according the same truth. Rather, God asks each of us to be true to ourselves—to create and live by our own code of morality and ethics.

Jesus Christ is no longer the one and only Son of God the Father who made heaven and earth. He wasn't born of a virgin, didn't live a sinless life, wasn't crucified for the sins of the world, didn't rise from the dead after three days, and most certainly could not have ascended to heaven before witnesses. No, Jesus Christ was merely a peasant philosopher and teacher. He thought deeply and worked diligently to make the world a better place, but he was just a man.

A Christian is no longer a person committed to loving God with all their heart, soul, mind, and strength and extending God's love to others. Instead, a Christian is someone on a journey of discovery who will hopefully remember the truth that has always been within their own heart—the "light within," according to the Gospel of Thomas—and simply live according to what is right to them.

A woman is no longer a person made (like all humans) in the image of God. She is an elite gender, daughter of a goddess, bearing the marks of the "divine feminine." Females, and females alone, have the ability to transcend the beastliness of men and matter.

A man is certainly no longer a person made (like all humans) in the image of God. He is an elitist power monger, unable to control his base desires and in terrible need, not of redemption, but of the balance that only a female can provide.

The Holy Grail is no longer the cup that Jesus drank from at his last meal with the people closest to him on earth. The Holy Grail is a woman, Mary Magdalene, who is not merely a follower of Jesus but the mother of Jesus' children—the one whom Jesus intended to lead his ongoing mission on earth after his death.

The church is not a group of fallible humans seeking to pursue an infallible God, nor is it the community of God intended to be light in a darkened world, providing hope and comfort to all who are weary. Instead it's a big business, engaged in the most massive cover-up in the history of the world, dedicated to protecting its own interests and power base, exercising control and domination over women, children, and anyone else it deems a threat to the good-old-boy network.

Some definitions can be debated, but there are also core issues, the details and definitions of which cannot be changed. Darkness is the absence of light. Error is the absence of truth. Cold is the absence of heat. Death is the absence of life. These are nonnegotiable terms. They mean what they mean or they do not mean anything at all.

Imagine waking up in a strange, new world where none of the words mean the same thing they used to mean. Stop means go, and up means down. You ask someone how they feel, and they say, "Orange!"

It's a nonsense world filled with things that don't make any sense, and you get the sickening feeling that someone designed it that way and is perpetuating this nonsense for some strange purpose.

This, in fact, is the gospel of Dan Brown: everyone gets to shape their own reality and none of it has to match. The definitions of all the key words have been changed. The concept of truth is outdated, history is obsolete, and the future is every man for himself.

True, Dan Brown did not do this alone. Not even he is that smart. The definitions have been changing on us, little by little, for the last hundred years. But with one novel, Dan Brown declared them changed to all intelligent, discerning readers of best-selling books worldwide. And thanks to the accompanying motion picture, moviegoers across the globe, who for some reason don't think the bodily resurrection of Jesus is believable but the bodily resurrection of Jason is, are also being sucked in. By redefining Christianity, Dan Brown can call himself a Christian while, as an "expert" on the subject, attacking the Christian faith. He has struck at the very foundations of what we believe, and we ought to be clearing our throats, because it's time for us to speak up. Most American Christians, realizing we are unequipped to rebut, have said nothing. Some Christians, recognizing the requirement of Jesus to demonstrate love if we are his followers, have done a very decent thing by trying to respond with kindness. However, we must remember that kindness without truth is not kindness at all. We'll unpack that idea more later in the book.

Let's compare the kind (but often truthless and toothless) response of the Christian community to *The Da Vinci Code* (and really, before that, *Angels and Demons*) with an incident that occurred almost a decade ago. Dan Brown frequently talks about religion as the enemy of science and progressive thinking, but he's not really talking about all religions. It's clear from his books that he's attacking the Christian religion. He never mentions Judaism or Buddhism. He certainly hasn't said anything negative about the religion of Islam. And this is for a very good reason: We're the only ones who let him.

Imagine what would happen if someone filmed a movie that portrayed Jews in a negative light. What if that someone claimed the film was based on a historically accurate account of Jewish religious officials conspiring to kill someone to protect their own base of power. What do you suppose would happen to that filmmaker?

Ask Mel Gibson.

Or suppose someone wrote a book suggesting that the holy book of the Muslims was corrupt. What if that book gave the impression that maybe Mohammed wasn't as much a man of God as people had been led to believe and that at least some of what he said may have been inspired by the devil? What would happen to that novelist?

Ask Salman Rushdie.

Thanking Salman Rushdie—An Islamic Response

We've seen how some Christians have responded to a book that assaulted the foundations of the Christian faith. How did the Islamic world respond to such a book?

In September of 1998, *The Satanic Verses* by Indian-born author Salman Rushdie was pre-released by its publisher. Before that year was over, the book had been banned in eleven Islamic countries. A month into the year after its release, the book (complete with effigies of its author) was burned in the Islamic community of Bradford, West Yorkshire, England (not too far from where the author lived). Protestors, before television cameras, carried RUSHDIE MUST BE DESTROYED! signs.

Perhaps someone should have told them it was just fiction.

In New York, the offices of Viking Penguin Books, which published *The Satanic Verses*, received seven bomb threats and thousands of threatening letters.[1] If Christians had responded similarly, they would have been called radical fundamentalists, which would have been an accurate description. And they would have been told repeatedly to calm down. After all, it's only fiction. But more than a decade later, Islam is being touted as a peaceful religion. It's the Christians who are murderous and untrustworthy.

What were Muslims so angry about? The "satanic verses" in Islam referred to a few words acknowledging the divinity of three birdlike goddesses who hovered somewhere between earth and Allah and could therefore intercede for the people. It is said by orthodox Muslims that these verses were added to the Qur'an and then removed and denounced as "satanic." Some western scholars claim that Mohammed wrote the verses and then, on second thought, took them out. In essence, he made a mistake. Orthodox Muslims hold that the verses were a complete fabrication, created by unbelievers early in the history of their religion.

Goddesses. Intermediaries. Disputed texts from early history. An attempted cover-up. Sound familiar? And there was more. One of Rushdie's protestors wrote this letter in explanation: "The book contains distorted, unfounded, imaginary and despicable material about the Prophet of Islam, and the Islamic history. The Muslim concept of God, the character and personality of the Prophet of Islam, the lifestyle of the Companions of the Prophet of Islam, the sanctity of Muslim institutions of prayers and pilgrimage, and many other areas of Muslim religion, culture and history have been ridiculed with the sinister motive of portraying millions of Muslims all over the world as barbarians."[2]

On February 14, 1989, just days before the book's actual release date, Iran's Ayatollah Khomeini issued a fatwa (legal declaration of a death sentence) over the radio: "I inform all zealous Muslims of the world that the author of the book entitled *The Satanic Verses*—which has been compiled, printed, and published in opposition to Islam, the Prophet, and the Qur'an—and all those involved in its publication who were aware of its content, are sentenced to death. I call on all zealous Muslims to execute them quickly, wherever they may be found, so that no one else will dare to insult the Muslim sanctities. God willing, whoever is killed on this path is a martyr."[3]

In response to Rushdie's assertion (through a work of fiction) that he no longer believed in Islam, Khomeini condemned Rushdie for the crime of apostasy, attempting to abandon the Islamic faith—an act punishable by death. On February 24, Khomeini promised a $3-million reward for anyone who would bring about Rushdie's death, and Rushdie went into hiding.[4]

Contemplating Salman Rushdie

Salman Rushdie actually gives us a lot to think about. Despite the obvious dissimilarities (Rushdie's award-winning, intellectual writing style versus Brown's "popular thriller"), some of the similarities in these cases are striking. For example, see Dan Brown's response to some of the allegations about his book:

QUESTION: Is this book anti-Christian?

DAN BROWN: No. This book is not anti-anything. It's a novel.[5]

(It is interesting that Brown falls back on the "it's only fiction" argument here—as if novels do not espouse the philosophy of their writers. Yet, he claims that nonfiction books of history do espouse their writer's philosophy. So according to Brown, novels are neutral; history is biased.)

SALMAN RUSHDIE (right after the burning of *Satanic Verses* in his own country): "The Satanic Verses *is not, in my view, an antireligious novel.*"[6]

QUESTION: The topic of this novel might be considered controversial. Do you fear repercussions?

DAN BROWN: I can't imagine why. The ideas in this novel have been around for centuries; they are not my own. Admittedly, this may be the first time these ideas have been written about within the context of a popular thriller, but the information is anything but new.[7]

SALMAN RUSHDIE (through his publisher): The author and Viking Penguin emphasized that *The Satanic Verses* was a work of fiction. Mr. Rushdie said that in one section of his novel there was a fictional prophet with a fictional name "subject to temptation." The incident from which the title of his book is taken is rooted in the early history of Islam. He noted that his novel included "a dream sequence, a fictional prophet and a fictional country"—and that he had gone to great lengths to fictionalize this sequence.

Mr. Rushdie said, "I studied history at Cambridge. The Islamic world would deny itself the techniques of scholarship and the imagination. If I wanted to write a purely religious history, I would not have written a novel."[8]

Islam, Christianity, and Fiction

Professor Paul Brians of Washington State University says, "It has been frequently claimed that serious fiction and art could largely fill the gap left by the collapse of the cultural influence of traditional religion. Fiction has not just been an irritant to religion in the West; it has posed itself as an alternative to it."[9]

We do take books pretty seriously in America. Short books and pamphlets from men like Alexander Hamilton, John Jay, and James Madison sparked the Revolutionary War. Later books, including *Uncle Tom's Cabin*, helped bring the abolition of slavery to the foreground of national debates. As stirring as a speech can be, the printed word has often led the way in America, igniting passionate action among young and old. Books are not neutral. Books can be inflammatory—and not just in America.

Some of the most volatile ideas in human history first found their way into conversations as a result of books. *Mein Kampf, The Kinsey Report, Beyond Good and Evil*—this list goes on and on. Even now, people continue to debate whether laissez-faire is the best attitude to take towards the writing, purchasing, reading and disseminating of books. Local libraries are still trying to figure out what to do with *Huck Finn, Of Mice and Men,* and *I Know Why the Caged Bird Sings.* Yet, as a general rule, the books we've listed were researched, written, published, and read in a context that has been heavily influenced by a Christian understanding of truth. If truth exists, and if Christianity is based on the ultimate claim of truth, then there is nothing to fear in any kind of research or philosophical speculation on truth.

This is important, so don't miss it: It is only within a relatively Christian context that ideas are considered worthy of exploration.

In non-Christian places, examination of well-known truths is not only discouraged but often violently opposed.

Descartes, Rousseau, Voltaire, Thomas Paine, Benjamin Franklin, Elihu Palmer—all wrote of ideas with consequences when taken to their logical conclusions.

But there's the rub. Few of us ever take an author's ideas to their logical conclusions. That would mean having to think outside the book. Instead, we read on and on, usually without much discernment. That kind of reading doesn't make us intellectuals. It makes us gullible, and, as a result, we've swallowed ideas whole without scrutinizing them. This is especially the case today when readers fall for the idea that our questions are more important than the answers. We can be an intelligent people, but we ought to be more careful—and more studious. We ought to start questioning ourselves about how much we really know.

Islamics don't really have a rich history of thought-provoking literature. They don't value literature the way we do. They don't hold that reason is more important than revelation, and they don't make darlings out of people who challenge the things they hold most dear. Their theology is erroneous, but you have to admire their conviction. Perhaps that's something we could learn from them.

Not that we're advocating book burning, which makes people look like fools and never actually stops the power of an idea anyway. And we certainly don't want anyone threatening Dan Brown's life. But let's show some conviction here. Leave Dan Brown alone personally but go after his ideas and rip them to shreds. They're paper-thin, anyway, so it's pretty easy to do. While scholars have done this in academic arenas, the average reader of novels isn't reading in academic arenas, so let's take it to the streets. Let's educate ourselves about the things that matter to the people we run across every day—the kinds of ideas that have sold more than 40 million copies of Dan Brown's last book.

Let's destroy the notion of a private faith that provides us with a personal hope that may be true just for us and show Christianity for what it really is: truth, founded on solid history, verifiable by the changed lives of people (historic and living), corresponding to nature and science, to beauty and goodness, to life and to what works. In an environment where our faith is shown for what it *actually is,* Dan Brown's book would have no impact at all. In a world where Christians actually lived out what they claim to believe, Dan Brown's books would be laughed at.

Consider one more item about Salman Rushdie and his book. It is said that after Khomeini issued his fatwa, Muslims began to consider their national identity secondary to their religious identity. Muslims (even children) no longer called themselves Egyptian or Pakistani; they were Muslim.[10] The Islamic community banded together. Some even began to think that traditional Islamic faith might take the place of communism as a formidable political force in the world. Their faith, and their enthusiasm, was rekindled.

We should be proud to be Americans, no doubt. In spite of all its flaws, the United States of America offers freedom, protection, and unprecedented opportunities. But we should be prouder to belong to Christ. Our U.S. citizenship must come second— a distant second—to our citizenship in heaven and our allegiance to Christ.

What have we done in response to Dan Brown and his books? Some bold and very thorough authors have made an accounting of the magnitude of error in Brown's books. Many have written and talked about the problems with Dan Brown's teachings. But thus far it looks a little like we're preaching to the choir, so to speak. Who's talking to the people out there who don't go to church, read Christian books, or visit Christian Web sites? How will we reach those that Christian churches and Christian publishing cannot reach?

That's where you come in.

What if regular folks who attend regular churches and work regular jobs just started living out what they say they believe? What if you started reading and thinking and talking to people about the real history of Western civilization and exposed Dan Brown's lies for a watching world? What if you did this with such calm and peace and love and generosity while still maintaining a firm and unyielding grip on truth that people just marveled? What if Christians could answer their critics without resorting to name-calling, book burning, and witch hunts?

In Search of Wonder

If we're going to thank Dan Brown for anything, let's thank him for leading us to consider Salman Rushdie, who (though definitely heretical in his own right) said a lot of really interesting things. Let's thank Dan Brown for making us aware that there is an intellectual and cultural elitism present in our world that believes human creations can take the place of God's—that our words carry equal weight with his words. As Mr. Rushdie said:

> *While the novel answers our need for wonderment and understanding, it brings us harsh and unpalatable news as well. It tells us there are no rules. It hands down no commandments. We have to make up our own rules as best we can, make them up as we go along. And it tells us there are no answers; or rather, it tells us that answers are easier to come by, and less reliable, than questions. If religion is an answer, if political ideology is an answer, then literature is an inquiry. . . . Literature is, of all the arts, the one best suited to challenging absolutes of all kinds; and, because it is in its origin the schismatic Other of the sacred (and authorless) text, so it is also the art most likely to fill our god-shaped holes.*[11]

We could spend all day talking about wonderment. Wonderment is the one thing postmodern culture doesn't hate. Wonder and an acknowledgment of the mysteries of life are two things written on our hearts that even the Enlightenment's misguided trust in human reason couldn't erase. Though our generation has more answers than any preceding generation—though we've witnessed discoveries in space, science, medicine, and technology that no one before us could have ever dreamed of—wonderment is still at the center of our being. It's what drives us to novels about the arcane.

Whether people realize it or not, every moment of wonder is a hunger for God. Even Rushdie recognizes that there are undeniable holes in people's hearts. We cannot let literary elitists pronounce their questions more important than our answers. Nor should we sit silently while they fill "god-shaped holes" with Silly Putty.

So what's a Christian to do? Talk. Christians can do this. If there's one thing Christians can do, it's talk. We sit in coffee shops. We have fellowship. We even invite our unchurched friends over to watch the game or have a cookout. But what are we talking about? We've got to start sharing our faith as real (personal, yes, but not by any means private) and start addressing the big issues of truth, goodness, and beauty.

WWJDWDB
(What Would Jesus Do with Dan Brown?)

So if we're not going to thank him, what *are* we going to do with Dan Brown? What would Jesus do with Dan Brown? He certainly wouldn't laud him for how hard he had worked researching his masterpieces. And while he epitomized kindness while on this planet, we don't find many examples in the Bible of Jesus apologizing to those who tried to distort his teachings. Apparently, Jesus had a different definition of kindness than we use. It's really hard to imagine Jesus—the one who was Truth personified—saying, "Well, I guess my truth just isn't true for him."

Jesus was kind. And Jesus certainly was not like some Christians today who seem to walk around spoiling for a fight. But there were limits with Jesus, and when someone came against truth because they thought they were better than it (think Pharisees), Jesus didn't back down. He didn't pull punches or apologize for regarding matters with the seriousness they deserve.

Undoubtedly, Jesus defines a lot of things differently than we do. Love looked a lot different after Jesus finished talking about it. So did life. And death. We wonder what he might actually do with our definition of kindness. Jesus could still be kind while telling you how wrong you were. He was kind and yet did not mince words when he said that if you didn't change your heart and mind about certain things, you would end up separated from God forever. He could do this because he really loved. His love guided everything he said. And when something needed to be said, he spoke. After all, how kind is it to know that someone is in terrible danger and not warn them? If you see someone poisoning the water system, kindness obligates you to do something, doesn't it?

What Made Jesus Really Mad

There were very few times during Jesus' life when he really got angry. We'll look at three in particular here, because they show a pattern. The first time Jesus enters the temple (John 2), he sees major corruption. To get you closer to his perspective, consider how impoverished people often made their pilgrimage to the temple once in a lifetime. They would scrimp and save their whole lives to finally make the journey to Jerusalem for a holy day, only to find animals being sold for sacrificial purposes at ridiculously inflated prices. These travelers would also have to exchange their money for proper currency and would be charged an inflated fee for the transaction. The high priest, Caiaphas, had quite a scam set up, taking advantage of the poor. In response, Jesus held his tongue, but he made his point pretty clear. He grabbed some rope, fashioned it into a whip, and drove the corrupt money changers from the temple.

The second instance of Jesus' anger was in the temple again (Mark 11). It had been about three years since he drove the money changers out. Since then, they'd returned. And now, they were taking advantage of foreigners. So Jesus turned his focus toward the commotion taking place in the court of the Gentiles. This was the only place a non-Jewish person knew to come and pray to the God of Abraham, Isaac, and Jacob. With all the animals bleating and customers haggling, no one could pray there. This was supposed to be a place of prayer for people of all nations. Jesus told them so, and they heard him loud and clear.

The third instance is in Matthew 23. The Pharisees had just tried to trap him and were secretly planning his death. Jesus delivered a message of eight *woes,* a word that carries the idea of pathos, anger, warning, and derision. He took the Pharisees to task for preventing people from finding God, for using their position to corrupt the faith of new converts and fleecing helpless widows, for swearing that they were telling the truth when they were lying through their teeth, for dressing up their selfish motives in religious doublespeak.

You're smart enough to see the obvious parallels in that last paragraph to Dan Brown. But look a little deeper. Look at all the times Jesus was really, really angry. Any time an outsider pretended to be an insider and used his position to keep others from becoming insiders, Jesus spoke up.

It's not hard to imagine that Jesus might want to have a word or two with Dan Brown.

Cursing the Ground While Walking on It

"Then we will no longer be infants, tossed back and forth by the waves, and blown here and there by every wind of teaching and by the cunning and craftiness of men in their deceitful scheming. Instead, speaking the truth in love, we will in all things grow up into him who is the Head, that is, Christ. From him the whole body, joined and held together by every supporting ligament, grows and builds itself up in love, as each part does its work" (Eph. 4:14–16).

In Ephesians, we are told to speak the truth in love. This means more than telling our Aunt Edna that we like her Spam, Velveeta, and Jell-O casserole when we don't or not pointing when your spouse has spinach in their teeth. What Paul tells us is that we *must not* sugarcoat the truth. We are *challenged* to speak against false teachings and not to let fear keep us from saying what is right.

We live in a Christian society and enjoy the freedom our citizenship in this land lavishes on us. Those critical of Islam in an Islamic country are deserving of death, according to their own religion. Rushdie's case is simply one rather high-profile example of this. Criticize communism in a communist society and, like Solzhenitsyn, you'll get imprisonment or worse. There are still martyrs for Christ in places like Indonesia, China, and the Sudan. But Dan Brown? He is only allowed the freedom he has because of what Christianity has bought him. Instead of suffering for his criticism of our faith, he's a multimillionaire precisely because of it.

We're sure Father John Sewell is a learned man, but he is only one religious person who happened to be quoted for the sake of the sell. His, and other quotes from clergy, are only more propaganda in the whirlpool that is our postmodern motherland.

So should we thank Dan Brown for his contribution? Emphatically, no! But neither should we declare a jihad. Our faith calls us to speak the truth in love, to *tell the truth* even if it's painful, to pray for our enemies and to bring light to the nations.

Chapter 8

DOES HE HAVE A POINT?

*E*ven a blind pig can find a truffle once in awhile—or so the old saying goes. Dan Brown is not a blind pig, and we're sure that what he's found is no truffle, but has the sweeping success of his last novel unearthed another hidden truth, one we've all needed to hear for quite awhile? Does the sales record of Brown's books say something about the state of our world and the failure of the Christian world to respond to it?

We think it does.

We think Dan Brown does have a point, but we think he takes that point too far. And we think that he offers a solution that is really no solution at all. *And* we think that his solution ultimately leads to disastrous conclusions. Still, he has a point.

You know it, and we've already said it: the church has not always done a good job of being God's redeemed community and redemptive force in the world. There have been times when Christians have not only been part of the problem, they've actually been the problem.

Some have suggested that the solution might be to get the church out of the world. So we Christians have created an alternative society we can live in. We have our own schools, our own radio stations, our own television networks, stores, books, movies, and theme parks. Many Christians live out their lives in Christian ghettos—never having anything to do with non-Christians. This, we were told at some point, will solve the problem.

But it hasn't.

We'll talk about this more in the next chapter, but for now just understand: Christians aren't doing the cause of Christ any favors by being narrow and intolerant or by producing inferior art and hanging it in the church's narthex. (We'll talk more about this later in another chapter.) Our walk needs to start matching our talk if we ever hope to solve the problems that plague our society. Dan Brown has a point: people don't trust the church. And we're going to have to earn the right to tell them they can.

Of course, the church is not the only place where lack of trust has increased during the last century. The failure of most political leaders to hold themselves to a high standard of ethics and morality (and the distrust that comes as a result of this) also helps Dan Brown sell books. The cover of the audio version of *Deception Point* is a picture of a mysterious iceberg draped in a shroud that bears the presidential seal. *Digital Fortress*, Brown's first thriller, features the NSA, the organization that protects all classified information that is stored or sent through U.S. government equipment. Brown's books appeal to something buried deep in the heart of the average reader —an alarming distrust of institutions in general, and of church and government leaders in specific.

As Christian Americans, we need to start holding ourselves to higher standards, choosing leaders with more integrity and setting about to make a difference in our country and for our Christian faith. If we really want people to believe the gospel is true, we're going to need to start demonstrating what it really is: a life-changing, empowering force that is strong enough to change not only our hearts and lives, but also our nation and our world.

Culture of Distrust

The identity of Deep Throat, the elusive inside source for the Watergate fiasco, has fascinated North Americans for more than thirty years. The media tried to decipher the code that would show why a group of government agents would try so diligently to dupe the people and cheat in an election they were going to win in a landslide in the first place. Finally, on May 31, 2005, ex-FBI operative Mark Felt confessed to being the mysterious mole inside the Nixon administration. For three decades, this man fueled the conspiracy theories of North American pop culture, urban legends, and political jokes. No wonder we are an untrusting people.

Let's face it: If our society was a trusting society, we wouldn't be reading *Angels and Demons* or *The Da Vinci Code* in the first place. Secret societies and conspiracy theories would probably bore us. If trust and trustworthiness were the norms, our relationships would be better and our communities would be stronger, and we'd all be so busy following our American dreams that we wouldn't have time to stop and read poorly written novels. But increasingly, we trust almost no one.

Many historians trace it back to the 1960s. John F. Kennedy's election as the thirty-fifth president of the United States signified hope for the American people. He was "one of us," raising his family in the White House and eloquently promising to get post–WWII America moving again—for civil rights, for science, for education. Americans, he said, could do more together than they could do alone. Under his leadership, it seemed we could conquer communism, poverty, and outer space and make the world a better, safer place all at the same time.

Kennedy's 1963 assassination, says Stephen Mansfield, was felt as "a collective trauma on an unprecedented scale, as though the whole nation had experienced a violent accident with all the fear, the uncontrollable emotion, and the desperate search for normalcy that follows such horrors." It left a "gaping national wound."[1]

The events that followed in this tumultuous decade continued to pour salt in those wounds. Vietnam was the first war in our country that didn't have the total support of the American people. And by 1965, more than 20,000 people were marching on Washington shouting, "Hey! Hey! LBJ! How many kids did you kill today?" Our trust in the office of the president was crumbling. The same year, events that led to race riots in Selma, Alabama, and Watts, California, demonstrated that though a newly passed Civil

Rights Act had made discrimination illegal, the battle for equality in this country was not over. Three years later, Martin Luther King Jr., the champion of the cause of equality, was shot dead by a sniper after calling his own country "the greatest purveyor of violence in the world."

And then there was Watergate, a cover-up that was worse than the crime itself. A country already reeling from pain was dealt a blow that may have been just too much to bear without turning cynical. As the conspiracy began to unravel, Nixon's press secretary, Ron Ziegler, stood before the press and lied. No covering that up. No attempt to divert our attention. It was just a lie. When this became evident, Ziegler stated an alternate position and followed with these words: "This is the operative statement. The others [the lies] are inoperative." To the time of his death in 2003, Ziegler still rationalized having lied to the press. "It's necessary to fudge sometimes. You have to give political answers. You have to give non-answers. But I never walked out on that podium and lied."[2] Fudging, non-answers, inoperative statements—apparently these are not lies.

Unfortunately for America, it didn't matter how Ziegler characterized what he had done. Americans now understood that the government could and did decide whether the truth was "operative" or "inoperative," and the downward spiral of public trust continued.

Mansfield explains: "Americans were beset by a nagging sense that they had been living a lie, that their patriotic ideals and symbols somehow masked a more greedy and viciously oppressive reality. The world had suddenly become a less certain, somewhat lonelier place."[3]

The '80s had the Iran-Contra affair, the debacle of Jim and Tammy Faye Bakker, and Ivan Boesky's insider trading, and anyone who lived through the '90s will likely be unable to forget the statement, "I did not have sexual relations with that woman."

In the 2000 presidential election, George W. Bush campaigned with a very effective ad that capitalized on this distrust. The tagline summed up the contrast between Gore's political philosophy and Bush's: "He trusts government. I trust you." The ad was so effective, that it ran in each of the "battleground states" for the duration of the campaign. Bush used the phrase in his final three debates and in speeches throughout the rest of the campaign.[4]

The decline in political trust that began in the '60s gained momentum as the decades rolled by. The year Bush won the election, polls showed that 60 percent of Americans believed the government would do what was right either "some of the time" or "never."[5] We have reason to believe it hasn't gotten any better in the years since.

Sadly, it appears we've experienced a total breakdown of trust in the people who lead us. We believe a lot in "agendas" and very little in the idea that our leaders have our best interests at heart. Corruption on the part of our leaders only feeds that suspicion. So what's the solution?

Americans seem to think that the answer is full disclosure about everything. Churches, educational institutions, and governmental agencies have often shrouded themselves in secrecy and made decisions behind closed doors, and for a long time, these were accepted practices. We aren't saying this is right in every case; we are merely saying this is how things have been done in the past. The popularity of Brown's books reveals a desire that maybe we missed before: people want to see us become more accountable—and rightfully so.

Previous generations fought *against* the public making decisions for an organization. Smoke-filled rooms behind closed doors where decisions are made are a caricature, but public opinion was definitely much less important to the way things were accomplished by institutions. Now nondisclosure means we're hiding something, and a decision made without taking public opinion into consideration is a decision that will not be easily accepted.

Following the events of September 11, 2001, and in the early days of the war on Iraq, Americans were screaming to have their questions answered: *Where are the troops? When are you going to attack?* Defense Secretary Donald Rumsfeld had a unique challenge when his job required him to remain silent before a generation demanding to be told. He basically had to say, "I can't tell you, or I'll also be telling the enemy."

When he continued to refuse to answer, Rumsfeld was accused of hiding something. Of course he was hiding something! That's what you do with information in times of war. Think of how bizarre it is that we would be willing to put national security and the safety of the men and women of the armed forces at risk just to satisfy our desire to know everything.

Becoming a Part of the Solution

The real solution is to select leaders of higher integrity not to demand higher levels of disclosure. Many people continued to support President Clinton in spite of his lying to the grand jury during the Monica Lewinsky scandal because, they said, his personal life didn't have an impact on his public life. As long as he continued to expand our economy, we didn't care if he committed adultery and lied about it.

Recently, we have seen the questioning of President Bush's nominees for the Supreme Court. The overriding sentiment seems to be that nominees should not allow their personal religious beliefs to impact the way they would rule in certain cases—the same argument made when President Bush named John Ashcroft as attorney general. Peter Berger characterizes this as a "dichotomization of social life." He says that contemporary society tends to view life in two categories: the public sphere (the government, academic institutions, large corporations) and the private sphere (church, family, and personal relationships).[6]

In other words, we are fine with our leaders being religious as long as that religion knows its place and keeps its nose out of the rest of a persons' life. This concept, however, is not religion—not really. Religion is best understood as a person's ultimate concern. If you want to know a person's real religion, don't look at his statements, look at what he thinks is most important—what he would be willing to give his life to, what occupies his thoughts, how he spends his time and money. This ultimate concern is his religion, and it will affect everything else about him—from the way he thinks about law to the way he thinks about education, art, and culture.

Once we understand this true concept of religion, we will not separate leaders into those who are religious and those who are not religious. We will understand that there is no such thing as a non-religious person. Instead, we will seek out those whose religion is trustworthy and able to address the real problems of a real society.

Dan Brown seems to say that power corrupts. But power doesn't corrupt; power merely reveals. Dan Brown has a point, but Dan Brown does not have a solution. A Christian worldview offers a solution. A Christian worldview says that yes, everyone is corrupt, but the gospel has the power to redeem corrupt people, transforming them slowly into people of integrity. The solution isn't to look to the fringes of Christian scholarship for a new faith. The solution is to look beyond the fringes to a real and transcendent source.

In his book, *Who Is My Enemy,* Rich Nathan addresses how Christians should go about engaging the culture and leading others toward that transcendent source. He proposes a four-point approach to speaking to others about our faith: we must be civil, we must be persuasive (not forceful), we must be realistic, and we must focus on the overarching themes of the Bible—namely, creation, fall, and redemption. If we can get past that first point, we're probably already over the biggest hurdle. Nathan cites former *Christianity Today* editor Carl F. H. Henry: "The real bankruptcy of fundamentalism has resulted not so much from a reactionary spirit . . . as from a harsh temperament, a spirit of lovelessness and strife. . . . This character of fundamentalism as a temperament, and not primarily fundamentalism as a theology, has brought the movement into contemporary discredit."[7]

As contrast to this unsympathetic spirit, Nathan tells of Francis Schaeffer, who could speak of culture with sharper insight than anyone in the Christian community in his time, but usually with a tear in his eye. D. A. Carson said of Schaeffer: "Whether or not one agrees at every point with his analysis, and regardless of how severe his judgments were, one could not responsibly doubt his compassion, his genuine love for men and women. Too many of his would-be successors simply sound like angry people. Our times call for

Christian leaders who will articulate the truth boldly, courageously, humbly, knowledgeably, in a contemporary fashion, with prophetic fire—and with profound compassion."[8]

That is the task ahead of us. As Christians, we must look at our fellows with compassion, recognizing the hurt on which their distrust is founded. At the same time, we must look to the transcendent source of all good things to find realistic ways to engage the culture in which we live. We must help restore belief in the existence of truth before we can even start to point toward that source of transcendent truth, and we should stick to the biblical story. At the same time, we need to take a long look at ourselves and our own levels of integrity and bring (or even become) leaders who win back the public's trust.

You Just Gotta Trust Me

In *24*, a popular gripping drama on TV, each season takes place within one twenty-four-hour period. Jack Bauer is the head of a top team of CTU (Counter Terrorism Unit) agents who uncover plots, rescue presidents, and, in the end, usually save the entire world from destruction. The episodes are riveting: What will the next hour hold? What will Jack Bauer do? How will he get out of this one?

If you're an avid *24* fan, you know that Jack Bauer has two key phrases that are repeated in almost every episode: "You don't have a choice" and "You just gotta trust me." If you watch the show and haven't noticed this, you will now. It's almost comedic, but this is how he gets the job done every time.

Here's a question: Why would someone trust anyone simply because he tells them to? Why would anyone respond to, "You don't have a choice" with "Oh, OK, yeah, of course. Sure. I get it. I don't have a choice. I'll do whatever you say. Blindly even." Why? Because it's Jack Bauer—rugged, handsome, brooding hero Jack Bauer. He's saved the world at least four times already. Why wouldn't you trust him?

First of all, this is television. We get it; it's fiction. But it's easy for a viewer to trust a character that has proven his worth through courageous action and rugged resourcefulness. But the writers of the show do not begin each episode (or each season for that matter) with a statement that everything you're about to witness is based on facts and research.

Dan Brown's stuff is fiction too, but he makes that statement (that his writing is based on facts and research), practically daring folks like us to write books like this. Still, why can this random writer with unreliable sources and no scholarly reputation whatsoever say, "You just gotta trust me," and actually get a positive response? It's almost like he backed it up with "You don't have a choice" and we buy it! "Oh, OK, yeah, of course. Sure. Jesus was married to Mary Magdalene. Why not? I'll believe what you say. Blindly even!"

We don't *want* to trust the people in authority in our lives and in our world, so we grab the first thing offered as an alternative. A little knowledge truly is a dangerous thing. By blindly following Brown's "trust me" sources, we have let cynicism and doubt take control of our lives—public and private. But it doesn't have to be that way.

Don't trust him. You *do* have a choice.

Chapter 9

RESPONDING WITH GRACE AND TRUTH

Grace makes beauty out of ugly things.
— U2, "Grace"

*H*ow are Christians to respond when someone like Dan Brown makes authoritative-sounding claims? As we mentioned in chapter 7, we certainly don't want to burn his books or call for his death like the Islamic community did to Salman Rushdie. Still, something must be done, and we are often at a loss as to what it is.

Should we challenge him to debate in the public square? Should we mock him and expose his research as fraudulent? Should we rally our troops with a passionate call to arms and a declaration that the culture wars are still ongoing?

Perhaps some variation of these responses is called for. But first, we should remember something significant: Jesus embodied truth. The Christ who walked the earth, God in the flesh, spoke truth, *was* and *is* truth. Anyone who claims to follow him must follow him in the way of truth and be prepared to defend the truth claims of Christianity.

But we must never forget that this divine Christ was and is *also* grace. The apostle John said it this way: "The Word became flesh and made his dwelling among us. We have seen his glory, the glory of the One and Only, who came from the Father, full of grace and truth" (John 1:14). Before we begin to formulate a proper response to the allegations made by postmodernists, skeptics, Gnostics, agnostics, or anyone else, we must make sure we are doing so from a posture of gentleness and respect. We must make sure that truth is always spoken in the context of grace and that our grace is always demonstrated in truth.

As followers of Jesus, we aren't merely concerned with getting into heaven when we die. We are also concerned with the ongoing work of transformation in this life. God's desire is to see his world restored. He has seen fit to perform this transformative work primarily through the lives of transformed individuals who are dedicated to going through life as Jesus would if he were in their shoes. "WWJD" is not just a bracelet and a clever marketing ploy; it is a reminder of the commitment we made when we turned over the leadership of our lives to him.

So in asking how we should respond to Dan Brown, we are really asking how Jesus would respond to Dan Brown. We touched on this briefly in chapter 7, but here we'd like to talk specifically about these two overarching themes of Jesus' life—grace and truth. Hopefully, by looking at Jesus' life and working through the lens of these two themes, we'll come away with a better understanding of how Christians can engage the culture in meaningful and effective ways.

Building Bridges and Turning on Lights

In the Bible, the truth is often associated with light. So, if Jesus came as the bringer of truth, you could say that Jesus came to turn on a light. But he also came as the bringer of grace—the one who could finally build a bridge between sinful people and a holy God. In other words, Jesus came to do two things: turn on a light and build a bridge. We have good reason to believe that these are the two primary tasks he wants his followers to engage in today.

It's important to remember the sequence: grace then truth. The reason for this is that people do not care how much you know until they know how much you care. It is one thing for Christians to stand aloof and uninvolved, wagging our fingers at a world that is going to hell before our very eyes. It is quite another to roll up our sleeves and get involved with that world. Anyone can stand on the sidelines and criticize, but Christ calls us to follow him into the melee, seeing people like Dan Brown, Elaine Pagels, and others not as the enemy but as victims of something bigger. Jesus died for Dan Brown and extends the offer of life everlasting to him just like he extended it to us.

Jesus came to the wealthy and powerful of his generation (like Nicodemus in John 3) and to the poor and scorned (like the Samaritan woman in John 4). He came to those who were looking for the Messiah (like Simeon in the temple or Nathaniel under the fig tree) and those who had no idea that a Messiah was imminent (like the Roman centurion). To each of these people, he brought his own unique brand of grace and truth—in that order.

Jesus the Bridge Builder

Jesus taught hard things. He once told a man to sell everything he owned to be a disciple. He said that the way up was down, and the greatest person in the kingdom of God would be the one who serves the most. He came up with the whole "turn the other cheek" thing and then showed us how it's done. He talked about all the things you're not supposed to talk about: hell, money, divorce, taxes. He challenged people in positions of authority and disrupted the status quo with his message and lifestyle. Like Philip Yancey says, "He wasn't Mr. Rogers with a beard."

But before he did any of that, before any of the teaching or any of the ethical mandates, he did something remarkable. He built a bridge. Before he gave us truth, he gave us grace.

Jesus lived before he was born. That's kind of hard to imagine, but it's true. He has lived for all of eternity and was there when everything that has been made was made. In fact, the Bible says that he was the One who created it all. It was all made for him and by him, and he is the One who holds it all together (Col. 1:17). Yet, for a short span of time, he actually entered into the world he fashioned and lived in it. Like an artist climbing inside his own painting, Jesus entered our world's time-space continuum and was—to some mysterious extent—subject to its laws and limitations.

He got hungry and tired and had to go to the bathroom. In fact, when he was born, he was not pretending to be a baby; he was a baby. The Incarnation was, among other things, scandalous. Jesus' humanity—his ordinariness—is what got him into trouble with the religious leaders of his time. He didn't act like they thought the Messiah should. He acted more like a real human.

The Incarnation: From Heaven to the Manger in a Heartbeat

The scandal of the Incarnation has produced more heresies than any other doctrine of the Christian faith. People can believe Jesus is God, but they can't believe he's human. Or they can believe Jesus was a man, but they can't believe he was also God. This is the central point over which Dan Brown stumbles, and the Bible clearly says that this doctrinal heresy must be confronted. We'll get to confronting heresy in a bit; but first let's make sure we're presenting an accurate depiction of the Incarnation ourselves.

A culture war went on in the early church between those who accented Jesus' divinity and those who stressed his humanity. And there were extremists on both sides. Dan Brown has merely sided with the extremists who stressed Jesus' humanity to the exclusion of his deity. Orthodox Christianity has always fought to maintain a both/and posture as opposed to an either/or. We need to make sure we haven't swung the pendulum too far in the opposite direction. After all, those are *our* sterile nativity scenes on display every December; those are *our* songs that suggest Jesus didn't cry when he was a baby ("Little Lord Jesus no crying he makes"). We bankrolled and watched the Jesus movies that have him floating around in a daze, speaking in an otherworldly tone. These are equally erroneous and must be corrected before we can ever hope to correct Dan Brown's error.

Perhaps we should take a refresher course in the humanity and humility surrounding the birth of Jesus as a means for understanding the grace we should be willing to extend to others.

Think back to the most comfortable place you've ever been. Remember the warm sun and the soothing sounds, the beautiful aroma of fresh-baked bread or roasting meat over an open fire, the knowledge that everything is under control, so there's not one thing to worry about? Have you ever been waited on hand and foot, surrounded by people telling you how wonderful you look, how wonderful you smell, how wonderful you are?

Do you have that in your mind? Label that place *A*.

Now, have you ever been to a working dairy farm? Remember those smells and those sights? You have to watch your step everywhere you go, and you might not want to touch some things without gloves on. Have you ever seen a feeding trough? The edges of them tend to be really smooth because of all the cow tongues that have lapped up every kernel of corn and grain and table scrap. Did we mention that cows do their business standing up, often while eating? The very fact that you would be looking at a cattle trough means you're probably standing in the waste created by the cattle.

Do you have that in your mind? Label that place *B*.

If you've ever seen a baby delivered, you know it's not a very noble way to enter the world. In our society, most babies are born in sterile hospital environments. Even with all our best medical technology, it's still a pretty gross experience—body fluids, mucus, blood, sweat, and screaming (and that's just from the dads).

Strip away all the modern technologies and comforts. When Jesus was born, there weren't any nurses or doctors with machines and medicine and clean linens. There were two peasants in a barn among the flies, barnyard animals, and manure. When God was born they wrapped him in strips of cloth and laid him in a feed trough. Think of that: the Author of Life, the King of kings, the Prince of Peace lying there among the spittle and leftover feed. That's the Incarnation. That's grace.

Think about this: in one moment, Jesus went from the most comfortable and beautiful place that has ever and will ever exist to one of the grossest, germiest places you can imagine. From *A* to *B* in a heartbeat.

Before he spoke a word, he built a bridge. He came from heaven to earth to make a way for us to get from earth to heaven. That's what we mean when we say that Jesus built a bridge. He brought us grace, and without grace there's no salvation. Without grace there's no hope. Without grace, there's nothing beyond the grave except misery and punishment and the full extent of human depravity without restraint in one, unending, monotonous, tortuous eternity.

That's where we were headed. And that's where we'd still be headed if it weren't for Jesus and the grace he provides. He built a bridge to make a way back for us to return to our heavenly Father. And after he built that bridge and demonstrated its ability to return us home, he turned on a light. It was after he came in humility, awkwardly learning to walk and talk and navigate life in our world, that he asked us to humble ourselves, awkwardly learning to walk and talk and navigate life in his world. He could ask us then. He had earned the right.

Turn on a Light

Jesus was meek and humble and gentle. But he wasn't a push-over.

Jesus yelled at people who were perverting the truth of his message. He was critical of how little faith his followers had even after they had witnessed miracles. He did not flinch when he told people that if they did not change their hearts and minds, they would end up separated from God forever. When people came and asked him questions, Jesus told them the truth. He knew that the stakes were high; eternities hang in the balance over matters of truth. We dare not be trivial in our pursuit of truth.

Our attempts to introduce people to Jesus will be ineffective if we do not first build that bridge. But we will still be ineffective if we fail to respond to honest questions with honest answers. That means a commitment to personal integrity first, but it also means a commitment to academic integrity.

Personal Integrity

We've bluffed for too long. We've pretended for so many years that it's sometimes hard to remember where the truth actually is. But those outside the walls of our churches know the truth about us. They know that statistics often prove that we divorce and lie and cheat on our taxes just as much as they do. They know that our kids get in trouble just like theirs do. And they know that we aren't everything we claim to be.

It's time to come clean. We did participate in witch hunts. No, not to the extent that Dan Brown and his misguided mythological research contends, but we were there. We did participate in the Crusades and the Inquisition. Again, the numbers are wildly inflated by postmodern historians, but it happened. We destroyed statues and shattered stained-glass windows in the wake of the Reformation. We burned books and cathedrals and people, and these were totally ungodly things to do.

Some of you might be tempted to think that, since those things happened centuries ago, we shouldn't bring them up here. If you prefer, we can mention more recent events. Many of our churches sat idly by while African Americans struggled to find equal treatment in this nation. We were the ones at the front of the bus. We were the ones with the fire hoses and dogs. We were the ones who snatched our kids out of public schools and created our own educational institutions because we didn't want "colored" kids corrupting our school system.

It's time to tell the truth about ourselves. Christians perpetrated hate crimes and racism, and we undermine our credibility when we try to deny it.

Of course, Christians are also responsible for most of the great art, music, literature, scientific, and technological breakthroughs.

Christians have fed the poor, clothed the naked, and housed the homeless. But we'll never be able to prove that if we aren't willing to own the serious mistakes of our past.

And that's what we're saying here. Many non-Christians are ready to hear the truth, but they're not interested in any half-truths from either side of the cultural debate. If we're going to tell the truth, we must tell the whole truth. In doing so, we stand a greater chance of being heard.

Academic Integrity

Once we have begun building bridges of grace and telling the truth about ourselves, we must be equipped to carry the conversation all the way through. We have to know history better than we do. We have to know science and art history and music and literature. We have to engage in rigorous academic pursuit, understanding that we are doing no favors to the cause of Christ if we continue the anti-intellectualism that has plagued contemporary Christianity for the last century.

It would be wise to target certain fields of study and encourage our young people to pursue those areas in a focused fashion. For example, where are the Christian artists of our time? We need Christian historians, biologists, composers, physicists, and economists. By this, we do not mean people who are both Christians and professionals. We mean people who approach these fields of knowledge from a Christian perspective, seeing all truth as God's truth and reclaiming the worlds of academia, the arts, and our government for the glory of God.

Just imagine a world where God's redeemed community is a beacon on a hill, a shining light overcoming the darkness of our world. Think about what could be if Christians took seriously God's invitation to partner with him in the redemption of not merely souls but culture as well. If we fought for academic integrity in our ranks with as much vigor and passion as we fight for political power, then we would be more likely to find a true seat of influence.

Perhaps sometimes we don't pursue academics because we think that they will lead us to truths that prove our faith wrong. But Christians need not fear. Study biology and you'll find more evidence for an Intelligent Designer than for random evolution. Study sociology and you'll find more evidence for natural law than for survival of the fittest. Study art and music and literature, and you'll find Christians who understood that creativity was a reflection of God's character and should be used to his glory. Unfortunately, you won't find as many in the last 100 years as you will in centuries past. But we can begin to change that.

Once we study and discover truth, it is not arrogant to state that truth. If we know that the New Testament documents are historically reliable, it's not a bad thing to say so; just like it's not bad to say that gravity is a universal force at work in our world or that objects at rest stay at rest unless acted upon by some outside force. Saying these things doesn't make us arrogant. But arrogance makes us say these things in ways that are impossible to hear.

The solution is not to deny the truths we have learned. The solution is humility. The solution is to remember that we are all saved by grace; none of us get saved by being smarter than other people. We all received truth from some transcendent source—none of us was smart enough to figure out the truth of God on our own.

Helmut Thielicke makes an interesting point in his book, *A Little Exercise for Young Theologians* (Eerdmans, 1999). He says that it's easy for young theologians to become arrogant because they know more about the Bible, theology, or ethics than others. He suggests that pride may be almost inevitable initially. But the antidote to this is not to stop learning. Rather, the antidote is to learn more. When it comes to learning about God, the more you know, the more you realize how little you really know. Good theology teaches humility, not arrogance, because good theology starts with grace and then adds truth.

Chapter 10

SHOOTING OURSELVES IN THE FOOT

Dear Friends,

I was on my way to the post office to pick up my case of free M&M's (sent to me because I forwarded an e-mail to five other people, celebrating the fact that the year 2000 is "MM" in Roman numerals), when I ran into a friend whose neighbor, a young man, was home recovering from having been served a rat in his bucket of Kentucky Fried Chicken (which is predictable, since as everyone knows, there's no actual chicken in Kentucky Fried Chicken, which is why the government made them change their name to KFC).

Anyway, one day this guy went to sleep and when he awoke he was in his bathtub and it was full of ice and he was sore all over and when he got out of the tub he realized that HIS KIDNEY HAD BEEN STOLEN. He saw a note on his mirror that said "Call 9-1-1!" but he was afraid to use his phone because it was connected to his computer, and there was a virus on his computer that would destroy his hard drive if he opened an e-mail entitled "Join the crew!"

He knew it wasn't a hoax because he himself was a computer programmer who was working on software to prevent a global disaster in which all the computers get together and distribute the $250.00 Neiman-Marcus cookie recipe under the leadership of Bill Gates. (It's true—I read it all last week

*in a mass e-mail from BILL GATES HIMSELF, who was also
promising me a free Disney World vacation and $5,000 if I
would forward the e-mail to everyone I know.)*

*The poor man then tried to call 9-1-1 from a pay phone
to report his missing kidneys, but a voice on the line first asked
him to press #90, which unwittingly gave the bandit full access
to the phone line at the guy's expense. Then reaching into the
coin-return slot he got jabbed with an HIV-infected needle
around which was wrapped a note that said, "Welcome to the
world of AIDS."*

*Luckily he was only a few blocks from the hospital—the
one where that little boy who is dying of cancer is, the one
whose last wish is for everyone in the world to send him an e-
mail and the American Cancer Society has agreed to pay him a
nickel for every e-mail he receives. I sent him two e-mails and
one of them was a bunch of x's and o's in the shape of an angel
(if you get it and forward it to more than 10 people, you will
have good luck, but for only 10 people you will only have OK
luck, and if you send it to fewer than 10 people you will have
BAD LUCK FOR SEVEN YEARS).*

*So anyway the poor guy tried to drive himself to the
hospital, but on the way he noticed another car driving
without its lights on. To be helpful, he flashed his lights at him
and was promptly shot as part of a gang initiation.*

*Send THIS to all the friends who send you their mail and
you will receive 4 green M&Ms. If you don't, the owner of
Proctor and Gamble will report you to his Satanist friends and
you will have more bad luck: you will get sick from the sodium
laureth sulfate in your shampoo, your spouse will develop a
skin rash from using the antiperspirant which clogs the pores
under your arms, and the U.S. government will put a tax on
your e-mails forever.*

I know this is all true 'cause I read it on the Internet.

Ever get one of these? Or the particularly "Christian" one
(with the baby angel graphics hovering in the background) that

says some poor child is sick, and if you love God, you will pray for
the child and send the message to at least ten people (the impli-
cation being that if you don't send it, you must not love God).
They've become so common that there's actually a Web site (www
.breakthechain.org) that features a "Sick Child Hoax-O-Matic."
It's a fill-in-the-blank form that uses a random boy's name and a
body part along with several other key words. In less than a second, you can have your very own Sick Child e-mail to send to all
your friends.

Unfortunately, Dan Brown isn't totally off base when he portrays the Christian community as being naive and undiscerning.
Sometimes we just don't think. Like when we put catchy slogans
up on our church signs that say really trite things that we (somehow) think are clever: "God answers knee-mail," or this summer-
time favorite, "You think it's hot out here," followed up by "The
Son can prevent you from burning!" or "Our church is prayer-
conditioned."

How do you suppose that sounds to a nonbeliever? Do we
expect to hear in someone's testimony one day: "I was driving by
the church building and saw your sign. I thought to myself, *I do
think it's hot out here. Obviously, hell is going to be hotter than this, so
I should probably go in there and give my heart to Jesus.*" We've never
heard that. Have you?

Neither have we ever heard a waitress tell us, "The reason I first
came to church is because Christians are always the best custom-
ers I have. They never complain. They always tip generously. I love
Sunday lunch because of all the noncomplaining, generous-tipping
Christians I get to wait on." We've never heard that testimony either.
Have you?

As Christians, we are often our own worst enemies. The world
watches as we wade through scandals, abuse, cover-ups, deception,
intolerance. We shoot our own wounded and close ourselves up in
enclaves. We panic and believe the worst about people. We boycott
movies no one is really interested in seeing and ban books no one
really wants to read. We get upset over tiny issues (like how many

bad words were used in a particular movie) while allowing huge problems to go unaddressed (the plight of the homeless or the AIDS crisis in Africa). We allow ourselves to get distracted from our true mission (to be a redemptive force in our world) by chasing all these tiny tangents.

We go on television looking like hysterical Chicken Littles, claiming, "The sky is falling!" Then we wonder how anyone could possibly believe the crazy teachings of the new-age movement and why our numbers are shrinking. This part is really simple: until the church decides to get its own house in order, we will be ripe fodder for Dan Brown and conspiracy theorists everywhere, and we will dishonor the name of the one we represent on this earth.

What's Wrong with the World?

More than a century ago, the *Times* of London asked its readers for suggestions as to what was wrong with the world. The most succinct answer came from G. K. Chesterton. This brilliant writer submitted only two words: "I am." In other words, what's wrong with the world is not the non-Christians. It's not that there are too many liberals or feminists or Gnostics. What's wrong with the world is that Christians haven't been acting like people of God.

The reason the world is in the shape it's in is largely because of Christians who don't act like redeemed people set apart to love God and others for the sake of the world. That's what's wrong with the world. The real problem isn't that Dan Brown writes bad anti-Christian fiction or that Elaine Pagels writes bad anti-Christian nonfiction. The real problem is that the church has not been living out its calling in such a compelling way as to cause people to view Brown's and Pagels's assertions as laughable.

So we're going to offer three things we must stop doing if we're ever going to engage the culture in meaningful and relevant ways. We've got to stop being foolish. We've got to stop being tacky. And we've got to stop being mean.

Stop Being Foolish

Sometimes we look foolish. And it's not because of our belief in the virgin birth or the bodily resurrection; sometimes it's because of our belief in things like Proctor & Gamble's ties to the satanic church. It's because we send money to television quacks who promise us that if we will just sow a seed in their ministry, sickness will not be allowed in our homes.

When ABC's *Prime Time Live* did an exposé on Robert Tilton back in November 1991, they found prayer request letters in the trash dumpsters. When confronted with this information, Tilton responded, "I laid on top of those prayer requests so that the chemicals actually got into my bloodstream, and . . . I had two small strokes in my brain."

What?!

We're not in a position to judge anyone's salvation here. And we've all done silly and downright foolish things. But come on! These things contribute to an overall negative image for Christians. They present obstacles and barriers for people who might otherwise actually want to investigate the claims of Christianity. Many people wonder, *If I become a Christian, does that mean I have to become like them?*

The impression a lot of people have in their heads is that in order to become a Christian, one has to park one's brain at the door. Anyone want to guess why that's the impression they have? They didn't make it up on their own.

We dishonor God when we fail to love him with our minds and our manners. When we forward Internet hoaxes, when we give the waitress a gospel tract instead of a tip, when we call for a boycott of the Teletubbies, we're not helping the cause of Christ. We're giving people a reason to think that Christians are foolish. And we dishonor our Christian friends when we see them advocating this kind of garbage and don't call them on it.

If we're going to present a picture of Christianity that is winsome and attractive, we've got to stop being foolish. We've got to use our brains, do our homework, and live lives of intellectual integrity. So let's settle this issue once and for all. Let's just resolve to stop doing things without thinking. If we are among those who forward superstitious e-mail versions of urban legends, let's vow to stop. No more "Madelyn Murray O'Hair is trying to shut down TBN" e-mail forwards. For crying out loud, the e-mail never even spells her name correctly, and the poor woman's been dead for years! Stop sending that e-mail. Proctor & Gamble does not have ties to the satanic church, Janet Reno does not think you're a member of a cult, and no one wants to steal your kidneys.

Stop Being Tacky

Have you ever considered what the average non-Christian thinks when he sees our WWJD boxer shorts hanging in the store or our "Jesus Saves" air freshener? Dave Burchett wrote a provocatively titled book, *When Bad Christians Happen to Good People.* In it he mentions one particular witnessing tool that upset him: "How about the Gospel Fly for bringing your unchurched, unsaved friends to the faith? The Gospel Fly is a fishing fly to be worn on your lapel that will make you a fisher of men. When your friend asks you what kind of fly that is on your lapel (which would happen to me constantly), you are instructed to reply, 'This isn't a fly for fish. It's a fly for making me a fisher of men.' Or an optional gender modification for women is to call it a people fly. Oh, by the way, in the suggested script, your nosy friend is referred to as a fish."[1]

A few years ago, there was actually a singing Mother Teresa doll available in some Christian bookstores. You could wind her up, and she would sing "You Light Up My Life." We're not making that up.

Sadly, it's not just a few misguided crazies participating in these kinds of activities; it's our friends. Sometimes it's the same nice people who are cooking food for the elderly and the sick. Sometimes it's our own pastor.

Where are the Handels of the Christian community now? Where are the Rembrandts? Where are the Dostoyevskys? (Perhaps stuck in front of their computers sorting through the junk e-mail we've sent them.)

We understand that there are Christians artists out there who are working hard to produce good work to the glory of God. But we must confess: good Christian art is still the exception rather than the rule. Christian trinkets and knickknacks are, unfortunately, still the rule.

Stop Being Mean

It is a sad but true fact that some of the meanest people we've ever known are among those who knew the most Scripture. It's as if they believe that spiritual maturity equals intolerance of others. They're not righteous; they're self-righteous.

Jesus was sinless, and yet he was the most approachable person who ever lived. Completely righteous in every thought, word, and deed, but so likeable that hookers, tax collectors, and the marginalized all felt comfortable approaching him and telling him anything. Sinners liked to hang around Jesus. They don't always like to hang around his followers. Why is that?

We use the language of a holy war a lot, acting like our primary goal is to destroy those who don't think like we do. Our primary goal should be redeeming culture and bringing healing and salvation to hurting and confused people. Perhaps we are too quick to point the finger at our unbelieving neighbors for the troublesome times in which we live. If we are going to win the culture wars (and we do believe there *is* a war going on), we're going to have to stop shooting our own wounded and stop shooting ourselves in the foot. In fact, Jesus might say we're going to have to stop shooting, period. This war will not be won with violence, whether in word or deed, thought or action. This war will be won with love. Not hysteria. Not money. Not political power.

Cal Thomas and Ed Dobson helped create the Religious Right. After several years, however, they began to be disillusioned by the abuses of power they saw. For example, they noticed a particular pattern in the approach used to raise funds. First, an enemy would be named Democrats, liberals, abortionists, homosexuals, Hollywood, or some combination of all of them. Then, the enemy would be accused of being "out to get us" by imposing their values on the rest of us. Next, the fund-raising letter would assure the reader that something would be done to ensure that this enemy would not be allowed to take over the country. Finally, supporters would be told that "if you really want to make sure we're successful, you can help by giving money."[2]

Not only is this approach completely unbiblical (Jesus never taught his followers that the biggest problem in the world was a corrupt national government), it brings out the worst in us. It fosters the idea that sin is somewhere *out there* instead of *in here*—inside the church and inside our hearts. Establishing an us-against-them mentality encourages us to draw lines and view people on the wrong side of the line as our enemy instead of as a slave of the enemy to be loved and pursued. It's easy to demonize the other side, but, as Kenneth Bailey says, "Blessed is the movement that is willing to listen to a courageous voice quietly insisting, 'There are devils among us and angels among them.'"[3]

Some Helpful Suggestions

It is said that Voltaire was considered the wisest man of his age. People were always clamoring for his attention, asking for an audience with him, and trying to get his opinion and advice on any number of topics. It reached a point where he could hardly keep up with the demand, so he struck upon an idea. He would limit those who could meet with him by putting a rule in place. He declared that he would meet with anyone as long as the conversation was in Latin.

For too long this has been the stance of the church. We will welcome anyone who will come to us, speak our language, and behave properly. Until you can do that, we're not really interested in having

you around. We have practiced a strategy of isolationism, withdraw-
ing from society and creating our own parallel subculture.

This stands in sharp contrast to what Jesus actually had in mind.
John 17 shows that, the night before he died, he prayed to his Father,
"My prayer is not that you take them out of the world but that you
protect them from the evil one. . . . As you sent me into the world,
I have sent them into the world" (John 17:15, 18). Jesus calls us to
go into the world and be a leavening force—not just an evangelistic
force but also a redemptive force for the culture. To be that force, we
must become students of the culture, harnessing when it is timely
to say what is timeless. We must stop making the world learn our
language; we must go and learn theirs first. As Art Lindsley, senior
fellow at the C. S. Lewis Institute says,

> *It is good to be able to state the other person's position*
> *to his or her satisfaction not only so that you might more*
> *effectively counter it but also to be fair. We value the dignity of*
> *people made in the image of God. When you counter someone*
> *in a dismissive, hostile or belligerent manner, you violate his*
> *dignity. Even when you do not particularly respect the person*
> *you are talking to, it is important to value the image of God*
> *in her. James 3:9–10 argues, in effect, that we cannot go to*
> *church and bless God, then walk out the next minute and*
> *curse someone made in the image and likeness of God. There is*
> *a relationship between the worth you ascribe to God and the*
> *worth you ascribe to people made in his image. . . . Our call is*
> *to love not only our neighbor but also our enemy. It is essential*
> *that we bend over backwards to be fair to people we oppose.*[4]

Christians must get involved in politics, in academics, in the
stock market, in medical research, in entertainment. Christians
should lead the way in every field of endeavor. Christians should be
the experts, the ones who have invested the most time and energy
in the best research and produced the best results. If we were living
like this, no one would question the validity of the gospel's power to
transform individual lives and societies at large.

Rearranging Chairs on the Titanic

Unfortunately, many Christians have been given the impression that involvement in life on this planet isn't worthy of their attention, that the only activity worth their time on earth is evangelism. After all, millions of people are on their way to hell unless they hear and respond to the good news. But is there futility even in engaging directly in public life? Is it as pointless as rearranging chairs on the *Titanic*?

C. S. Lewis talks about this in his essay "Learning in War-Time." He agrees that winning souls is more significant in the long run than redeeming culture, but there can't be an either/or approach to this. It's impossible for a person to completely divorce himself from life on this planet in a particular culture. We practice evangelism in a specific context and cannot suspend our cultural lives in favor of some higher spiritual life. It's just not possible.

Lewis, like the apostle Paul, compares the Christian life to military service. He writes: "Neither conversion nor enlistment in the army is really going to obliterate human life. Christians and soldiers are still men. . . . If you attempted, in either case, to suspend your whole intellectual and aesthetic activity, you would only succeed in substituting a worse cultural life for a better. You are not, in fact, going to read nothing, either in the church or in the line: if you don't read good books, you will read bad ones. If you don't go on thinking rationally, you will think irrationally. If you reject aesthetic satisfaction, you will fall into sensual satisfactions."[5]

Soldiers do not spend every hour of every day fighting. They sleep. They eat. They play cards, watch movies, write letters home, shower, and find time to toss a baseball around. Christians, likewise, aren't going to spend every second telling others about Jesus. Nor should they think of this as some kind of ideal to strive for. Christians are supposed to engage in other activities. No amount of passion for the priority of the gospel can prevent them from cooking, cleaning, reading, watching, relaxing, and caring for what God has entrusted to them. Instead of trying to run away from these "normal" activities—which we can't do anyway—we should realize that there are no "normal" activities if we do them to the glory of God. We must figure out how to cook, clean, read, watch, relax, and care "in the name of the Lord" (Col. 3:17, 23).

Doing these things well should actually enable us to be more effective in our evangelism. For years, well-intentioned Christians have reduced the gospel to "fire insurance," telling their unbelieving friends and neighbors that the good news is that you don't have to go to hell; you can go to heaven when you die. We've acted as if the only concern people have is what's going to happen to them after they die.

But what troubles most of the people we know, what keeps them awake at night, has more to do with having to live here and now. When we reduce salvation to getting into heaven when we die without addressing the purpose of our lives on earth (beyond recruiting others to join us in heaven), we don't help people understand what true discipleship is (and we don't make it any easier for them to believe our message and become disciples in the first place). This could be why so many new converts continue living the same old way they always have, reading the same books, having the same marital problems, watching the same movies, running up the same amount of credit-card debt they did before they met Jesus. If nothing matters until we die, why bother?

But what if we reminded people that Jesus wanted to redeem everything about them? What if Jesus really *is* interested in absolutely every aspect of life from the way we drive to the way we shop to the way we close a business deal? What if we believed that Jesus wasn't just interested in rescuing us from hell in the next life but that he also wanted to transform everything about life starting right now?

Instead of being assaulted (and insulted) by our offers of cheap fire insurance, intelligent and thoughtful unbelievers might actually be impressed by the power of the gospel. Rather than thinking that Christians are so heavenly minded as to be of no earthly good, they will know that it is our heavenly perspective that drives us to excellence in all areas of our life here below.

As C. S. Lewis reminds us, the best poets, philosophers, artists, and architects *should be* Christians who model the creativity and charity of our Creator. The finest musicians and mathematicians should be people of faith, who draw upon the order and organization of the Intelligent Designer of us all. What would unbelievers think if, every time they looked for an expert's opinion, that expert turned out to be a Christian, regardless of the field? How might the world be different if the best novelists, the best sound engineers, the best accountants, the best stock analysts, and the best physicians (and maybe all the nicest people) all operated within the framework of a Christian worldview?

That might not be enough to cause unbelievers to embrace the truth about their sin, but it could, at least, be a demonstration of the power of the gospel to transform individuals and societies. Before we can expect people to accept our faith, we must show them that it actually works in our homes, on our jobs, and through our expressions of thought. We should be careful to avoid saying that our faith is true because it works. But we should be able to demonstrate that it *does* work because it *is* true.

William Wilberforce and the Power of the Gospel

One of the greatest examples of the power of faith to change the world ever was British abolitionist William Wilberforce. Millions of people have been influenced by this man's tireless efforts to end slavery. He exposed the hideousness of slavery, intending to lead men away from the practice of it, not necessarily toward Christianity. But his life and work in parliament has influenced many.

Early on, Wilberforce almost gave up his career in politics. Right after he became a Christian, he assumed he would have to sacrifice his political ambitions. If he was really going to be committed to the cause of Christ, he thought, he would have to serve God by becoming a pastor or evangelist.

Thankfully, he sought out the wise counsel of John Newton (author of the hymn "Amazing Grace" and a former slave trader who became a powerful preacher). Newton told Wilberforce that his clear and thoughtful voice of conviction and reason might be put to better use in the halls of government where he already had a position of influence. It wasn't long after this meeting with Newton that God laid upon Wilberforce's heart the notion of abolishing the slave trade. Wilberforce spent the next twenty years trying to convince his fellow legislators that stopping slavery was a moral imperative. It took another twenty-six years to end slavery altogether, but it happened—three days before Wilberforce died.

More than any sermon preached by John Newton, Wilberforce's life presents a powerful testimony to the earth-shattering power of the gospel. Why did he believe that freedom should be the inalienable right of all ethnicities? Why did he believe that human life is intrinsically valuable and that ending slavery was a moral imperative? Wilberforce fought for these things because he embraced a Christian worldview.

So if the best public speakers, the best lawmakers, the most well-respected and sought-after thinkers in the realm of public policy and human rights were Christians, what message would that send to a skeptical world? And how viable would Dan Brown's gospel be in that context?

Chapter 11

NICAEA

Most folks understand that Dan Brown is a real person and Robert Langdon is a fictitious character. Vittoria Vetra only exists in a novel *(Angels and Demons)*; Constantine existed in history. Teabing is fake. Leonardo da Vinci is real.

But what about Jesus?

The actual existence of Jesus of Nazareth, like that of Buddha, Abraham, and King David, *has* been disputed. There was a famous instance in the nineteenth century when Bruno Bauer suggested that Jesus only existed as "an idea." In 1910, Arthur Drews suggested that Jesus was just the "Christ myth" repeated so many times that he became real in our minds.

These are both extreme views, and for the last hundred years, no reputable scholar has denied the historical existence of Jesus. But there are plenty of people who want us to believe that the Jesus who *did* exist was very different from the Jesus we have heard and read about. They want us to believe that Jesus was just a wise man, a revolutionary prophet, *a* man of God but not *the* man of God—and certainly not the *Son* of God.

Real author Dan Brown's fictional character, Teabing, tells another fictional character, Sophie, about a historical gathering known as the Council of Nicaea. Fictional Teabing tells fictional Sophie that this is where and when the historical Jesus of Nazareth became the fictional God Incarnate.

Separating the Facts from the Spin

Confused? Let's take a look at Jesus of Nazareth and the Council of Nicaea and try to separate historical fact from Dan Brown's fiction.

Really, it's not as complicated as Mr. Brown would like us to believe. Jesus of Nazareth belongs to history. He entered the world at a certain time in a certain place for a certain purpose. According to the New Testament, he was born during the reign of the Roman emperor Augustus and the rule of King Herod. Augustus ruled from 27 BC until AD 14 and Herod from 27 BC until 4 BC. This gives us the window of time in which Jesus physically came into the world.

According to the Roman historian Tacitus and the New Testament Gospels, Jesus died while Pontius Pilate was governor of Judea (AD 26–36). This gives us the window of time in which Jesus physically left the world. Jesus was probably born in the winter of 5 or 4 BC and died in AD 29.

Like many other ancient events, the specific dates of Jesus' birth and death are not known specifically, but generally. What seems of primary importance to the New Testament writers is not *when* it happened as much as *that* it happened.

Jesus was Jewish. He lived in a small, poverty-stricken outpost of the Roman Empire. There are no legal documents about him. If he was registered in any of the court files of his day, record of it has not survived. He lived a short life, even by first-century standards, of about 33 to 36 years. Most of his life was spent in quiet obscurity. His public ministry lasted approximately three years (based on the three annual Jewish Passover feasts which are recorded in the Gospel of John).

We have no reason to believe that Jesus traveled to India or England or the New World, as some authors have posited. It appears that his life and work were restricted to his own country—with the exception of a brief time in his childhood spent in Egypt. Most of his adult life was spent in the secluded northern territory of Galilee and in Jerusalem.

And yet this one man has been the single greatest influencing factor in the history of the human race. His impact is felt so greatly that people divided human history into two parts: the part before him and the part after him. According to David Barrett's figures in the *World Christian Encyclopedia*, somewhere between 25 and 33 percent of the people on earth consider themselves Christians. Jesus transcends culture; Christianity is found in 8,100 different ethno-linguistic peoples, and Christian literature is now published in more than 2,000 languages.

Jesus didn't leave a single word written down. In fact, the only time we know of Jesus writing anything, he was scribbling in the dirt, and we have no idea what it was.

That means we have to rely on other sources for information about what he said and did. Some of those sources are contemporary Roman and Jewish historians, who don't tell us much, other than that Jesus actually existed and that some people considered themselves followers of his teaching.

The main sources we have are the four Gospels contained in the New Testament, which are considered by most scholars to be the original testimony of the Christian faith. The word *gospel* means "good news," so these four books are not to be thought of as biographies of Jesus. They don't tell us much about his whole life. We know nothing of his early thinking or education. We don't know a lot about his personality or whether he liked spicy foods or not. The writers of the Gospels share some common themes and ideas and demonstrate differences in tone and emphasis in their presentations of Jesus.

The overarching idea, however, is that Jesus of Nazareth is more than a carpenter, more than a teacher, and more than a brilliant thinker. Jesus of Nazareth is the long-awaited Messiah, the incarnate Son of God.

The Gospels aren't objective, scientific histories. They were written by people with an agenda. That's obvious, and we don't deny it. These writers believed in Jesus and had been radically and fundamentally changed because of their beliefs. His life and teaching and death and resurrection had altered their personal histories; and they knew it would alter the course of human history as well. For them, Jesus was not just a dead hero; he was alive and present and active among them. So these writings are not merely reports of what happened; they are declarations of faith intended to incite faith in others. One of the most powerful statements made in each of the Gospels is that, somehow, the man Jesus was also *Immanuel,* which means "God with us."

This is the cornerstone of the Christian faith. According to the New Testament, there is plenty of room for debate on the finer points of Christian doctrine. But no one can deny the full deity or the full humanity of Jesus without renouncing Christianity.

What has the Christian church traditionally believed about Jesus? Was he God or human or both?

The first Christians were Jewish. As such, they believed that "the Lord our God is one Lord." But by the time of the birth of the Christian church at Pentecost, the early followers of Christ had come to refer to Jesus as "Lord." The Gospels demonstrate how gradually, because of Jesus' life and teaching and his resurrection from the dead, his early disciples realized he was the Son of God, and the long-anticipated Messiah whom Jewish people expected to come and deliver them from the hands of their oppressors.

The early church used various titles to describe Jesus, such as Redeemer, Savior, Lord, and Son of God. Clearly, they held a high view of Jesus. Perhaps the most exalted statement regarding Jesus' nature is in the prologue to John's Gospel. Any educated Jew or Greek reading this at the time would have understood the author's intention to link Jesus with the divine: "In the beginning was the Word, and the Word was with God, and the Word was God. He was with God in the beginning. Through him all things were made; without him nothing was made that has been made. In him was life, and that life was the light of men. The light shines in the darkness, but the darkness has not understood it. . . . The Word became flesh and made his dwelling among us. We have seen his glory, the glory of the One and Only, who came from the Father, full of grace and truth. . . . For the law was given through Moses; grace and truth came through Jesus Christ" (John 1:1–5, 14, 17).

The apostle John wanted people to know that Jesus of Nazareth was a human being and was God at the same time. Dan Brown wants us to believe that Jesus wasn't considered divine until the Council of Nicaea in AD 325. He suggests that Constantine manipulated the bishops there to "vote" for Jesus' divinity for political purposes. He also says it was a relatively close vote.

We think John's statement above is not only indicative of his personal belief but is descriptive of how *most* early Christians thought of Jesus years before the council of Nicaea had gathered.

The apostle Paul was another real person and he wrote plenty of documents that we still have today. Few, if any, reputable scholars would argue against Paul's writings being dated between AD 48 and AD 67. That's even before the apostle John wrote his Gospel. Paul was a contemporary of Jesus who converted to Christianity within a decade of Jesus' death. Nero eventually had him executed in AD 67, and his writings are essential components of the New Testament.

If, as Dan Brown asserts, Constantine hijacked Christianity in the fourth century, reinterpreting the life, mission, and message of Jesus, then we should find direct contradictions between the Nicene Creed and Paul's writings. But we don't.

Paul says that Jesus was a man with a human mother (Gal. 4:4). In the very same verse, he says that Jesus is God's Son. Later, Paul would say that Jesus was "being in very nature God" (Phil. 2:6). Paul claims that Jesus is the "Lord . . . through whom all things came" (1 Cor. 8:6) and that Jesus "is the image of the invisible God . . . by [whom] all things were created" (Col. 1:15–16).

So, we have one eyewitness in the apostle John, and we have one of the earliest Christian writers in the apostle Paul. And from them to the time of Nicaea, we can trace a straight line of people whose writings remain today and clearly state that Jesus was more than a human, being God in the flesh.

- Ignatius (AD 105): "God Himself was manifested in human form."

- Clement (AD 150): "It is fitting that you should think of Jesus Christ as of God."
- Justin Martyr (AD 160): "The Father of the universe has a Son. And he . . . is even God."
- Irenaeus (AD 180): "He is God, for the name Emmanuel indicates this."
- Tertullian (AD 200): "Christ our God."
- Origen (AD 225): "No one should be offended that the Savior is also God."
- Novatian (AD 235): "He is not only man, but God also."
- Cyprian (AD 250): "Jesus Christ, our Lord and God."
- Methodius (AD 290): "He truly was and is . . . with God, and being God."
- Lactanius (AD 304): "We believe Him to be God."
- Arnobius (AD 305): "Christ performed all those miracles . . . the . . . duty of Divinity."[1]

We're not trying to say that everyone who claimed to be a Christian understood Jesus to be both human and divine. What we are saying is that such a belief was normal and not, as Dan Brown suggests, the invention of the Council of Nicaea.

It's hard to say exactly what most people understood as orthodoxy in the first 200 years of church history. For the first couple of centuries of its existence, Christianity was considered a *religio illicita*—an illegal and forbidden religion. The agenda for them was survival, so they had little time for theological debates or the formulation of detailed arguments about their faith. Initially, converts were mostly Jewish (or at least familiar with the fundamentals of Judaism) and operated easily within the framework of Jewish thought, sharing common sensibilities as well as a common vocabulary.

Heretical sects began cropping up from the very beginning, offering differing ideas and standards of orthodoxy. At first, the differences may have seemed minor, but as years turned to decades and decades turned to centuries, those differences became more and more pronounced until they constituted completely different renderings of the faith. The two most common areas of distinction were in the areas of *Soteriology* (how a person receives salvation) and *Christology* (the nature, character, and actions of Jesus Christ).

It is the area of Christology that most concerns us here.

In direct contrast to Dan Brown's assertions, the first heresy of the church was not that Jesus was merely human, but that Jesus was merely divine. Ignatius of Antioch argued strongly that Jesus was a real person with flesh and blood because a sect called the Docetists was claiming that Jesus only *appeared* to be human but was really a divinity in human disguise.

Later, a group called the Ebionites declared that Jesus was merely human, although the supreme prophet.

Even later, a group called the Adoptionists thought Jesus was a very holy man who was "adopted" to the position of God's Son at his baptism.

New Christians and the Need for Clarity

After the Edict of Milan (AD 313) made Christianity a legal religion and offered Christians the full protection of the law, churches began to receive a new influx of converts almost immediately—many from polytheistic backgrounds.

Converting to Christianity from paganism during this period would show several things about you. For one, you would have been a very religious person. Everyone at the time knew that the *pax Romana* (peace of Rome) was dependent upon the *pax deorum* (peace of the gods). Even Cicero wrote in *On the Nature of the Gods* (I.3), "If our reverence for the gods was lost, we should see the end of good faith, of human brotherhood, even of justice itself."

Another thing this would mean is that you would have believed religion to be mostly made up of ritual-keeping. As long as you performed your religious rituals properly, it didn't really matter what you believed.

And you may still have held to polytheism, regardless of your Christianity. Everyone (except the Jews) believed in many gods. One god may have been your family's god, but you may have worked somewhere that called on you to pay homage to a different god. This was the norm. You didn't give up one god for another. You added the worship of one god to the worship of another. As D. H. Williams explains in *Evangelicals and Tradition,* "You accrued religious benefit not by rejecting previous gods and former allegiances in order to embrace new ones but rather by accumulating multiple deities and participating in the various worship services offered to them."[2]

Christianity was vastly different. Becoming a follower of Christ meant following him only. Monotheism's exclusivity would be new to you. It would feel strange. So would the idea that your religious activities were less important than the allegiance of your heart and mind. "In other words," D. H. Williams says, "the content of one's faith mattered; simply performing the right services was not enough."[3]

Other Gospels

As the Gospels and epistles were being written and circulated during the time of the apostles, the early church was being instructed and established on the foundation of apostolic teachings and writings. It wasn't until the second and third centuries that other gospels about Jesus began to circulate. Dan Brown says there were eighty of these non-canonical gospels, but the number was substantially smaller. As the Jesus movement began to grow, more and more people wanted to get in on the act, and one of the best ways to do that was to write a story about Jesus and slap an apostle's name on it. Most of these forgeries have crazy stories in them, like Jesus making real, live pigeons out of clay or Jesus pushing a little boy off a roof or Jesus coming out of the tomb followed by a giant, dancing cross (we're not making this up).

There was a lot of confusion, and the early church leaders realized that they needed to have some kind of consensus on how an illegitimate writing was to be distinguished from an authentic one. And they did come up with criteria by which they could evaluate these different documents. To make it into the official New Testament canon, a writing had to have ties to an apostle (like Matthew, Peter, Paul, or John), it had to be consistent with the teachings of

Jesus, *and* it had to have been considered authoritative by the church for a long time.

Dan Brown discusses other ancient books about Jesus' life and suggests that the church was trying to cover them up. But you can't cover up something that doesn't exist, and these later gospels didn't exist in the first century. They reflect later Gnostic thought and are inconsistent with apostolic time and certainly with apostolic doctrine. For example, here's an actual quote from the much talked about Gospel of Thomas: "Simon Peter said, 'Let Mary leave us, for women are not worthy of life.'

"Jesus said, 'I myself shall lead her in order to make her male so that she too may become a living spirit resembling you males. For every woman who will make herself male will enter the kingdom of heaven'" (Gospel of Thomas, 114).

This is clearly unlike anything else Jesus says in the New Testament.

It took awhile, and there were a few books that people waffled on (though none of the Gnostic gospels even came close), but the contents of the New Testament we have today are the materials that fit the standards mentioned above. The idea that what we have today in the New Testament is a result of Constantine putting it all together in AD 325 for political purposes is ridiculous. More than 100 years before Constantine, Origen said, "Matthew to be sure and Mark and John as well as Luke . . . only four Gospels are recognized. From these the doctrines concerning the person of our Lord and Savior are to be derived. I know a certain gospel which is called *The Gospel according to Thomas* and a *Gospel according to Matthias* and many others have we read—lest we should in any way be considered ignorant because of those who imagine that they posses some knowledge if they are acquainted with these. Nevertheless, among all these we have approved solely what the church has recognized, which is that only the four Gospels should be accepted."[4]

Again, that's a quote from more than a century before Constantine and the Council of Nicaea. And, as it turns out, this isn't even the biggest issue Christians had to deal with. In Harry Gamble's

Books and Readers in the Early Church, Gamble suggests that the illiteracy rate of the general population of the Roman Empire was nearly
90 percent. So most Christians were functionally illiterate, meaning
they couldn't have learned about Jesus by reading a genuine Gospel
anyway.[5] Most Christians would have learned by the way Paul advo-
cates in Romans 10:17, "Faith comes from hearing the message."

Any value Christians placed on the written word (and they did
value the written word from the very beginning) was superceded by
the need for a way to transmit the elementary principles of the faith
through confessions and hymns.

Defining the Faith at Nicaea

Thankfully, by the fourth century, the church didn't have to
worry about struggling for survival. Theologians began to formulate
systematic doctrine and construct simple, memorable creeds that
could be memorized and recited by all believers. They did this for
two reasons: (1) they needed to and (2) they could.

The "need to" was twofold. First, they wanted to correct error.
Second, they wanted to instruct new believers—including one
rather high-profile new believer named Constantine. So they began
to sit down together and hash out what they believed the original
orthodoxy was. Their goal was to both defend and define the faith.

The primary error that the Council of Nicaea took to task was
one being spread by Arius. Arius believed that the Father is the only
true God; the Son is of an entirely different status. In other words,
Arius believed that the Son was a created being. Athanasius, who
was the bishop of Alexander at the time, strongly opposed Arius by
pointing out a number of devastating consequences to Arius' dangerous theory. Athanasius' argument went like this: (1) No creature
can redeem another creature; true redemption must come from the
Creator. (2) According to Arius, Jesus Christ is a creature. (3) Therefore, according to Arius, Jesus Christ cannot redeem humanity.

Unfortunately, the pendulum swung too far in the opposite
direction, and the next heretical theologian of note was Apollinarius

who argued that Jesus could not be considered totally human. He was opposed by Gregory of Nazianzus.

At this point, Constantine intervened. Brown portrays the emperor as a master manipulator, using Christianity to his own political purpose. Maybe that accusation is justifiable; maybe it's not. Constantine's conversion may not have been entirely sincere, but he was a masterful politician who recognized that schisms of this magnitude would constitute a destabilizing force in the empire. If that sounds too cynical, we could give Constantine the benefit of the doubt and say that, having committed himself to Christianity, he wanted, understandably, to know exactly what he was supposed to believe.

Whatever the reason, it was he who called together more than 300 church leaders from across the empire—primarily from the east—to gather at Nicaea (in modern-day Turkey) in the summer of 325, asking them to come up with a clear statement of belief. The fact that most of the bishops in attendance were eastern should have been favorable to Arius' cause. That was where he had the most influence.

People traveled for thousands of miles to attend the gathering. The Arians submitted their statement that Jesus was merely a creature and must have had a beginning with this famous statement from their leader: "There was [a time] when He [the Son] was not."

The Council recognized the incongruity between this idea and the combined teaching of all of the accepted Gospels of the church. According to Arius, there was no sense in which Jesus could be called God. If Jesus wasn't God, he couldn't redeem fallen humanity. A creature cannot redeem a fellow creature. He believed that the New Testament writers referred to Jesus as God in name only and that he did not share in the nature of God.

Arianism was officially condemned, and Arius was exiled when he refused to move from his heretical position. The bishops drew up a statement based on the writings of the New Testament that affirmed Jesus' divinity. This had been, after all, the historic position of the church for nearly 300 years. The new creed was adopted by a final vote of 316 to 2—not quite the close call Dan Brown asks us to believe it was.

The result is remembered as the Nicene Creed, which originally looked like this: "We believe in one God, the Father, almighty, maker of all things visible and invisible; and in one Lord Jesus Christ, the son of God, begotten from the Father, only-begotten, that is, from the substance of the Father, God from God, light from light, true God from true God, begotten not made, of one substance from the Father, through Whom all things came into being, things in heaven and things on earth, who because of us men and because of our salvation came down and became incarnate, becoming man, suffered and rose again on the third day, ascended to the heavens, will come to judge the living and the dead; and in the Holy Spirit."

Dan Brown seems to think that the Council of Nicaea settled things once and for all. Ironically, the Nicene Creed had little impact immediately other than to heighten the awareness of the issues at hand. For the next twenty-five years or so, it didn't really accomplish what Constantine had hoped.[6] It wasn't until the Council of Constantinople in 381 that the Nicene Creed was given the polish it needed to become the enduring orthodoxy for the church that is still recited around the world today:

I believe in one God, the Father Almighty, Maker of heaven and earth, and of all things visible and invisible.

And in one Lord Jesus Christ, the only-begotten Son of God, begotten of the Father before all worlds; God of God, Light of Light, very God of very God; begotten, not made, being of one substance with the Father, by whom all things were made.

Who, for us men and for our salvation, came down from heaven, and was incarnate by the Holy Spirit of the virgin Mary, and was made man; and was crucified also for us under Pontius Pilate; He suffered and was buried; and the third day He rose again, according to the Scriptures; and ascended into heaven, and sits on the right hand of the Father; and He shall come again, with glory, to judge the living and the dead; whose kingdom shall have no end.

> *And I believe in the Holy Ghost, the Lord and Giver of*
> *Life; who proceeds from the Father and the Son; who with the*
> *Father and the Son together is worshiped and glorified; who*
> *spoke by the prophets.*
> *And I believe in one holy catholic and apostolic Church. I*
> *acknowledge one baptism for the remission of sins; and I look*
> *for the resurrection of the dead, and the life of the world to*
> *come. Amen.*

Considering the Question Yourself

The most important question you must answer is not what fictional characters like Teabing or Robert Langdon think about Jesus. The real question isn't even what real people like Dan Brown or the Council of Nicaea think about Jesus. Ultimately, the question you have to deal with is, What do you think about Jesus? Is he just a human? Is he just a god? Is he somehow both?

If Jesus of Nazareth were not God, then you'd have to think him insane. After all, he does claim to be able to forgive sins (Mark 2:1–12). Could one human have the power to do that?

In his book *Mere Christianity*, C. S. Lewis asks his readers to answer that question. Rather than paraphrase him, we thought we'd give you the entire quote and challenge you to chew on it for awhile:

> *One part of the claim tends to go unnoticed because we*
> *have heard it so often that we no longer see what it amounts*
> *to. I mean the claim to forgive sins: any sins. Now unless the*
> *speaker is God, this is really so preposterous as to be comic.*
> *We can all understand how a man forgives offences against*
> *himself. You tread on my toe and I forgive you, you steal my*
> *money and I forgive you. But what should we make of a man,*
> *himself unrobed and untrodden on, who announced that he*
> *forgave you for treading on another man's toes and stealing*
> *other men's money? Asinine fatuity is the kindest description*
> *we should give of his conduct. Yet this is what Jesus did. He*

told people that their sins were forgiven, and never waited to consult all the other people whom their sins had undoubtedly injured. He unhesitatingly behaved as if He was the party chiefly concerned, the person chiefly offended in all offences. This makes sense only if He really was the God whose laws are broken and whose love is wounded in every sin. In the mouth of any speaker who is not God, these words imply what I can only regard as a silliness and conceit unrivaled by any other character in history.

Yet (and this is the strange, significant thing) even His enemies, when they read the Gospels, do not usually get the impression of silliness and conceit. Still less do unprejudiced readers. Christ says that He is "humble and meek" and we believe Him; not noticing that, if He were merely a man, humility and meekness are the very last characteristics we could attribute to some of His sayings.

I am trying here to prevent anyone saying the really foolish thing that people often say about Him: "I'm ready to accept Jesus as a great moral teacher, but I do not accept His claim to be God." That is the one thing we must not say. A man who was merely a man and said the sort of things Jesus said would not be a great moral teacher. He would either be a lunatic— on a level with the man who says he is a poached egg—or else he would be the Devil of Hell. You must make a choice. Either this man was, and is, the Son of God: or else a madman or something worse. You can shut Him up for a fool, you can spit at Him and kill Him as a demon; or you can fall at His feet and call Him Lord and God. But let us not come with any patronizing nonsense about His being a great human teacher. He has not left that open to us. He did not intend to.[7]

Son of God or a lunatic? Able to forgive sins or not? One with God or one of the gods? The choice is all yours to make. But whatever you choose, we ask that you would choose wisely and not (like so many of Dan Brown's undiscerning readers) base your decision on the words of a character who, himself, doesn't even exist.

Chapter 12

BEYOND THE PALE OF ORTHODOXY

Inherit the Wind, by Jerome Lawrence and Robert E. Lee, was a fictionalized version of a historical event. And like *The Da Vinci Code,* it was told from a particular perspective. In this story, a substitute high school teacher is arrested for teaching Darwin's theories of evolution in the classroom. He is defended by a famous lawyer and prosecuted by a fundamentalist politician. It is a rather delicately masked interpretation of the "Scopes Monkey Trial" (1925) with debates between William Jennings Bryan and Clarence Darrow concerning the same issue. But in this version, Bryan is represented as an arrogant, thick, closed-minded, intolerant individual. Darrow, on the other hand, is the voice of reason, the enlightened one pleading for tolerance in the face of narrow-minded fundamentalism. It is a gripping drama and it bears little resemblance to the real events that transpired that summer in Dayton, Tennessee.

Unfortunately, people don't remember the actual facts of the historical event. They remember the fiction (and the 1960 brilliantly cast movie version) and believe that it is history. The following is a conversation as it appears in the book (with pseudonyms attached):

DARROW ("DRUMMOND"): I don't suppose you've memorized many passages from *The Origin of Species?*

BRYAN ("BRADY"): I am not the least interested in the pagan hypotheses of that book.

DARROW ("DRUMMOND"): Never read it?

BRYAN ("BRADY"): And I never will.[1]

There are claims that this scene was taken almost entirely from the transcripts of the *State of Tennessee v. John Scopes* trial. But those claims are ridiculously false. In fact, Bryan read *The Origin of Species* many, many years before the trial ever took place. He did research, and wrote critical articles *based on that research*. But for the sake of the drama, we get some playwrights' manipulation of facts to fit their entertaining piece of propaganda. And it becomes especially emphatic when a famous actor like Spencer Tracey delivers the lines of the brilliant prosecutor.

Clearly, one of the marks of postmodernism is the blurring of lines—perhaps the eradication of lines altogether. However, we must make the following plea to writers, playwrights, and movie makers: If you're going to write fiction, write fiction and call it that. Please do not claim your fiction is based on history unless it actually is. Otherwise, people will believe you. And then when you are exposed, you will look like you had an agenda.

Of course, we are not naive. We realize that writers like Dan Brown know this already. We realize that Dan Brown has an agenda. And we do not believe that Dan Brown's agenda is to overturn the historically orthodox view of Christianity. Not even Dan Brown believes he can accomplish that.

We believe that the whole point of Dan Brown's writings is to prove to others that he is smarter than they are. He can figure out clever puzzles, and he knows history you don't know. He has read the real history (even though he'll also tell you that real history doesn't exist), and when you poke holes in his research, he falls back on the claim, "Hey, it's just fiction!"

There is nothing wrong with fiction. We love a good story as much as anyone. But what happens when a person isn't sure what they believe and the fiction ends up feeding them a particular belief system for lunch? That's when we have to ask writers to have some integrity and behave like responsible craftsmen.

Within Christianity, there has always been an acceptable amount of pluralism. That is to say, not all orthodox Christians believe the same things about every particular doctrine. There are disputable matters, after all. And certain doctrines are closer to the core than others. However, there are limits to this pluralism. There is an absolute somewhere. If there weren't, no one could truly follow the One who claims, "I AM."

So when people claim to be Christian, what exactly are they saying? More to our point, when Dan Brown claims to be a Christian, what exactly is *he* saying? Can he claim allegiance to the great I Am? Not if he has used the guise of fiction to confound thoughtful people and mislead them about their own faith, history, and the concept of truth overall.

Dan Brown says faith is a continuum. We say the Christian faith is set rock hard on a solid foundation of orthodox beliefs. Faith has its reasons, and faith—orthodox faith, at least—has its boundaries. Faith is a journey. Faith is lived within the context of ebb and flow. Faith often survives in the marrow between doubt and assurance. God is infinite, and measuring progress against infinitude is, needless to say, difficult if not downright impossible. But none of this negates the fact that something happened a couple thousand years ago. Time itself was split into two sections: before Christ and after Christ. That actual story of real Christianity must be remembered, not some fictionalized version of it.

Setting the Record Straight—Dan Brown's Jesus

Claims to Christianity

In sorting out precisely what theological position Dan Brown takes in *The Da Vinci Code, Angels and Demons* and (though in a lesser way) his other works, it may be helpful to consider what he explicitly claims regarding his own personal beliefs. We've mentioned this before, but on his official Web site, Mr. Brown reveals his true view of Christianity. For instance, he is asked, "This novel unearths some surprising Christian history. Are you a Christian?"

He responds: "Yes. Interestingly, if you ask three people what it means to be Christian, you will get three different answers. Some feel being baptized is sufficient. Others feel you must accept the

Bible as absolute historical fact. Still others require a belief that all those who do not accept Christ as their personal savior are doomed to hell. Faith is a continuum, and we each fall on that line where we may. . . . We're each following our own paths of enlightenment. I consider myself a student of many religions. The more I learn, the more questions I have. For me, the spiritual quest will be a life-long work in progress."

First of all, he dangerously left out one of the "answers" to what it means to be a Christian. He focused on the external markers and entirely left out the core of Christianity: a *relationship* with Christ. Granted, he wasn't exhaustive in his list, but the few that came off the top of his head are all works-based externalism and have nothing to do with what being a Christian actually is.

Furthermore, his viewpoint is really an old spin on new-age Gnosticism (as discussed in chap. 2), not orthodox Christianity. Notice that Brown deflects his answer by describing what *others* think being a Christian means, rather than what *he* believes it means.

What it means to be a Christian is not nearly as nebulous as Brown would have us believe. The Puritan writer Richard Baxter spoke of "mere Christianity," a term that C. S. Lewis used in his book of the same name. By "mere Christianity," we can speak of the traditional Christian creeds that orthodox, Catholic, and Protestant believers affirm, namely, the Nicene Creed and the Apostles' Creed, rather than Brown's "anything goes" aberration of Christianity.

An Alternative Religion

Let's go to *The Da Vinci Code* itself and open its pages again. But instead of taking it for face value, let's look at a few more of the "secrets" Brown's "enlightened" characters claim to know for sure:

- Jesus isn't like the four Gospels present him at all. He was married to Mary Magdalene, and they had a child whose descendants may still be alive.
- Jesus intended Mary Magdalene to be the head of the church after he died.

- This made Peter jealous, so he covered it all up after Jesus died.
- The early church engaged in a massive cover-up to conceal Jesus' marriage and his humanity in order to put men in control.
- Jesus was not considered divine until centuries after his death when the Emperor Constantine suppressed the ancient documents that tell the real story and had the Council of Nicaea cobble together what we have today as the New Testament.

Clearly, this book raises lots of questions for lots of people. Are there other ancient documents about Jesus besides the New Testament? Are they more reliable than what we have in the Scriptures? Was Jesus married? Was his wife Mary Magdalene? Did they have a child? Was Leonardo da Vinci part of a secret organization that knew all about this? Do we know why the New Testament includes only the books that it does? Was Jesus human or divine? What was the Holy Grail really? How much time would it take for us to sort all this out?

Here are our answers: Yes. No. No. No. No. No. Yes. Both. Who knows? About forty-five minutes.

Don't worry. We're not going to go into all these questions (but we highly recommend Darrell Bock's *Breaking The Da Vinci Code,* to provide even more insight into these questions). We're not going to talk about art or literary criticism (well, maybe a little). But if we are followers of this Jesus and holders of this faith, we must know for sure: *Does the Christian faith and our understanding of Jesus have a solid leg to stand on?*

Brown's hero, Robert Langdon, articulates the alternative religion that is promoted in this novel when he refers to Leonardo da Vinci and Saunière as sharing a "fascination for goddess iconology, paganism, feminine deities, and contempt for the Church" and claims that the Catholic Church sought to repress the idea of the sacred feminine. However, that claim is completely inconsistent with the Catholic Church's history and art.

For example, the veneration of Mary has been an important part of Catholic practice for centuries. In this painting, *Madonna Enthroned* by Giotto di Bondone (c. 1310), note the iconographic imagery from the Byzantine period. In it, Mary is portrayed as the Queen of Heaven with Jesus perpetually on her lap.

In this fifteenth-century painting by Fra Filippo Lippi known as *Madonna and Child with Angels*, the king's mistress' face is depicted as the face of the Virgin Mary. Everyone in the king's court knew this, and thus it was scandalous. But, once again, it illustrates the centrality of Mary in Catholic devotion.

Raphael's *Madonna and Child*, painted in the sixteenth century, shows a more familiar and accessible quality of Mary, but this again continues to illustrate the ongoing tradition of the veneration of Mary in the Catholic Church. In effect, these paintings are depictions of Catholic belief in "the sacred feminine."

While he makes many errors in the areas of art history, literature, biblical canonization, and church history, Brown is very adept at promoting the occult and goddess worship. After about twenty pages in, the novel becomes progressively propagandistic. In a quote

from his Web site, Brown answers this question: "This novel is very empowering to women. Can you comment?" His answer: "Two thousand years ago, we lived in a world of Gods [*sic*] and Goddesses [*sic*]. Today, we live in a world solely of Gods. Women in most cultures have been stripped of their spiritual power. The novel touches on the questions of how and why this shift occurred . . . and on what lessons we might learn from it regarding our future."

Two thousand years ago we lived in a world where a woman was not allowed to vote, own property, run for public office, or testify in court. Women were basically chattel. The Gnostic gospels, as we have seen, are far from empowering to women. If anything, they are the exact opposite. In one non-canonical gospel, death itself is blamed on women: "When Eve was in Adam, there was no death; but when she was separated from him, death came into being" (Gospel of Philip, 71).

Nothing has influenced the plight of women in their search for equal rights more positively than Christianity. The early church acknowledged women as key leaders from the very beginning: Phoebe (Rom. 16:1–2); Nympha (Col. 4:15); Priscilla (1 Cor. 16:19). Yes, the church has often failed to live up to biblical standards and has subjugated women at times, clearly ignoring the clear biblical teaching that in Christ there is no preferential treatment based on gender (see Gal. 3:28). Conversely, one has to twist the Gnostic texts in order to make them empowering to women.

Who Is Dan Brown's Jesus?

If, as Brown claims, Jesus was by no means divine, then why would anyone care about his supposed wife, Mary Magdalene, or about their progeny? What did Mary Magdalene ever say or do to show herself as anything other than an average woman? What significance has her alleged goddess-hood had upon any part of human history in the last 2,000 years? Who would have ever heard of her name today, had it not been for Jesus' interaction with her? The very idea that she is something special simply because she was married to Jesus ought to be offensive to women everywhere—giving the impression that a woman is not enough to merit our concern unless she is married to the right person.

Interestingly, Brown hypocritically deprecates Jesus' deity but elevates Mary as the sacred feminine—the true one worthy of worship. But Brown's reasoning simply does not meet his own standards, nor does it follow the obvious, verifiable facts of history.

The fact is, the clearest biblical image of the sacred feminine in Christianity is the body of Christ. We are his *bride*, which he is preparing for himself. And the ultimate marriage feast of the Lamb involves his union with that body, that *bride*. In this sense, we are all part of that "sacred feminine"—sacred in the truest sense of being set apart for his purposes.

Dan Brown's Jesus is not part of God at all; denial of Christ's divinity drives a stake through the heart of the Christian message.

Brown argues that, even though Christ's marriage isn't mentioned in Scripture, to be a Jew in good standing in that first-century community, one had to be married. This is patently false. Celibacy and singleness were somewhat exceptional, but were not forbidden by any social decorum or religious mandate. The Essenes are a perfect example of this. The first-century Jewish writer, Philo of Alexandria, described the Essenes as "those who repudiate marriage . . . for no one of the Essenes ever marries a wife." Significantly, the Essenes not only escaped condemnation for their celibacy but were often admired. Philo also wrote: "This now is the enviable system of life of these Essenes, so that not only private individuals but even mighty kings, admiring the men, venerate their sect, and increase . . . the honors which they confer on them." Citations like these clearly reveal that not all Jews of Jesus' day considered marriage obligatory. In fact, those who sought to avoid marriage for religious reasons were often admired rather than condemned.

Several of the prophets were single: John the Baptist, Jeremiah, Elijah, and Elisha. The apostle Paul also made it clear that marriage was optional. He wrote, "I think that it is good for you to remain as you are [as a virgin]. . . . Are you unmarried? Do not look for a wife" (1 Cor. 7:26–27). Incidentally, if Mary Magdalene were married to Jesus, we would expect him to show special concern for her at the cross as he did with his mother. But he did not.

As we noted earlier, Scripture does teach that Jesus will be married, but his bride will be his church. The church is the body of believers who have entrusted themselves to Christ for forgiveness and newness of life.

The True Jesus

Christianity's Claims

"They all asked, 'Are you then the Son of God?' He replied, 'You are right in saying I am'" (Luke 22:70). All of the Gospels support and affirm the full deity of Jesus Christ. And these documents are primary historic documents that are well-attested by early manuscripts and patristic quotations.

The first-century New Testament epistles (the letters of Paul and others) also teach the deity of Christ and affirm this again and again. For example, Paul in Colossians 2:9 says, "For in Christ all the fullness of the Deity lives in bodily form." And in Titus 2:13, he uses the phrase, "the blessed hope—the glorious appearing of our great God and Savior, Christ Jesus."

Theologians continue to debate the finer points of Christian doctrine, but there are a few key beliefs without which one cannot really be considered a Christian. One cannot be a Christian without believing that Christ was somehow both God and man.

The primary historical documents that comprise the New Testament reveal the identity of the true Jesus. Again, Colossians 2:9 tells us, "For in Christ all the fullness of the Deity lives in bodily form." It is Jesus, both the human *and* the sacred, that makes our belief what it is.

John 3:16, probably the most famous verse in the Bible, says, "For God so loved the world that he gave his one and only Son, that whoever believes in him shall not perish but have eternal life." The statement, "For God so loved the world" reveals the Father's love for his people. He is not a distant, abstract deity. He is not impersonal. He is very personal, so much so that he desires intimacy with us in spite of the alienation caused by our rebellion against his loving intentions for our lives. We try to avoid these claims because of our quest for autonomy and independence. In spite of our rebellion against God's good purposes for us, he was willing to undergo the greatest of pain, the boundless pain of sending his only begotten Son into this world.

God is a relational being. In the mystery of the divine Trinity, the Father, the Son, and the Holy Spirit are three co-equal and co-eternal persons, yet one God who has always enjoyed perfect communion and mutual love. In fact, God is a community of being. It is out of the superabundance and the overflow of his eternal love that he created us as creatures who could respond to his loving initiatives—moral agents who could enter into communion with him.

At the core, Dan Brown seems to know very little about what it means to have the attitude of Christ Jesus, who, "being in very nature God, did not consider *equality with God* something to be grasped, but made himself nothing, taking the very nature of a servant, being made in human likeness. And being found in appearance as a man, he humbled himself and became obedient to death—even death on a cross! Therefore God exalted him to the highest place and gave him the name that is above every name, that *at the name of Jesus every knee should bow,* in heaven and on earth and under the earth, and *every tongue confess that Jesus Christ is Lord,* to the glory of God the Father" (Phil. 2:5–11, italics ours).

I AM's love is a perfect and holy love. He cannot compromise his own character and have fellowship with imperfection. Thus, the alienation caused by the Fall had to be overcome.

No Alternatives

Robert Langdon says to Sophie, "Every faith in the world is based on fabrication" (*DVC,* 341). It is true that the other religions of this world are all variations of works systems. Their followers attempt to achieve nirvana, satori, enlightenment, heaven, or a right relationship with God through their own merit, through their prayers, through their giving, or through their sacrifice.

The Scriptures, however, reveal a God who is so holy and perfect that the standard of perfection is manifested in the character of his Son. In the incarnation, God took humanity into himself and became the God-Man. The result was that in Christ Jesus, his offer for our sakes, his sacrifice on our behalf, was a perfect gift of grace that we could never hope to merit, earn, or achieve. If that is fabrication, folks, there is no reason to pick a faith at all. Eternity and existence and basic belief turn into profoundly sad futilities.

But John 3:16 says that "whoever believes in him shall not perish but have eternal life." The word *believe* (*pistuo* in the Greek) means more than intellectual assent. It also means personal, volitional reception. To believe in this sense is to transfer your trust from your own merit to the merit of Christ Jesus and his perfect work on our behalf. To receive a gift, you cannot get it merely by believing it is there, or by believing that someone wants to give it to you. Something more is required. We need to reach out and accept that gift. When we accept this gift by receiving Christ and inviting him into our lives, we are given eternal life, which is a new quality of life—the life of Christ. This life makes us perfect and acceptable in the eyes of God, because he sees the righteousness of Christ in us.

Brown Inherits the Wind

Brown says he is a Christian, but he is very selective in his use of early religious documents. He chooses to completely ignore the consistent witness of the New Testament epistles, even though a number of these epistles predate the Gospels. He also ignores the affirmations of deity in the writings of the pre-Nicene church fathers. For example, in the early second century, Ignatius of Antioch wrote of "our God Jesus, the Christ." Many such affirmations can be found throughout the writings of the church of the second and third centuries.

Additionally, in contrast to what Brown suggests, there is plenty of non-Christian testimony from the second century that Christians believed in Christ's divinity. In a letter from Pliny the Younger to the Emperor Trajan, dated around 112, Pliny said that the early Christians "were in the habit of meeting on a certain fixed day . . .

when they sang . . . a hymn to Christ, as to a god." It is clear that Christians believed in the deity of Christ well before the Council of Nicaea. It is these historical references and an understanding of what Christianity is all about that prove most of *The Da Vinci Code*'s theories about Jesus and the early church as patently false.

But Brown continues to harangue the Christian church through the character Teabing, who says, "By officially endorsing Jesus as the Son of God, Constantine turned Jesus into a deity who existed beyond the scope of the human world, an entity whose power was unchallengeable." He goes on to say that "the early church literally *stole* Jesus from His original followers, hijacking His human message, shrouding it in an impenetrable cloak of divinity, and using it to expand their own power" (*DVC*, 233). He says further that "Jesus was the original feminist. He intended the future of His church to be in the hands of Mary Magdalene" (*DVC*, 248).

Teabing adds that, "almost everything our fathers taught us about Christ is *false*" (*DVC*, 235). . . . Nothing in Christianity is original" (*DVC*, 232). And that "'until *that* moment in history, Jesus was viewed by His followers as a mortal prophet . . . a great and powerful man, but a *man* nonetheless. A mortal.' 'Not the Son of God?' 'Right,' Teabing said" (*DVC*, 233).

Finally, he claims that "the early Church needed to convince the world that the mortal prophet Jesus was a *divine* being. Therefore, any gospels that described *earthly* aspects of Jesus' life had to be omitted from the Bible" (*DVC*, 244).

Sweeping claims like these are simply sub-scholarly. The canonical Gospels indeed affirm the earthly aspects of Jesus' life. It is the Gnostic gospels that do not. It is critical to note that the claim that the early church suppressed the Gnostic gospels is completely false, since these documents *did not exist* until the late second century and third century. It is impossible to suppress something that does not exist.

It is ironic that Brown has Teabing say, "What happens if persuasive scientific evidence comes out that the Church's version of the Christ story is inaccurate, and that the greatest story ever told is, in fact, the greatest story ever sold?" The irony here is that, based on its popularity, it is Brown's book that appears to be one of the greatest stories ever sold. His evidence is specious. It is not new; it is not persuasive; and it is certainly not scientific. He would do well, by contrast, to consider the real, historical Jesus. The real Jesus is both prophet *and* the Son of God. The biblical response is aptly summarized in the old quote often attributed to Dwight L. Moody: "If you want to know how crooked a stick is, put a straight stick down next to it."

We are instructed by biblical writers to not be sucked in by ungodly notions. Paul urges the Ephesians in 4:14–15 to "no longer be infants, tossed back and forth by the waves, and blown here and there by every wind of teaching and by the cunning and craftiness of men in their deceitful scheming. Instead, speaking the truth in love, we will in all things grow up into him who is the Head, that is, Christ." James 3:15 tells us that false teachings involve "such wisdom [that] does not come down from heaven but is earthly, unspiritual, of the devil."

Collin Hansen in *Church History* magazine says, "Though unoriginal in its allegations, *The Da Vinci Code* proves that some misguided theories never entirely fade away. They just reappear periodically in a different disguise. Brown's claims resemble those of Arius and his numerous heirs throughout history, who have contradicted the united testimony of the apostles and the early church they built. Those witnesses have always attested that Jesus Christ was and remains God Himself. It didn't take an ancient council to make this true. And the pseudo-historical claims of a modern novel can't make it false."[2]

In our own view, if this book were about any other subject than finding fault with Christianity, it is unlikely that it would have become a best-seller on the basis of academic or literary merit. Unfortunately, in our culture, trying to punch holes in traditional Christianity is now an acceptable way of placing oneself on the highway to popularity and financial success. One doesn't dare bash Muslims, African Americans, females, homosexuals, or any other group protected by the guardians of political correctness. Numerous beliefs and lifestyles are crooked sticks, but the straight stick of Christianity is not even picked up to be tested against them. It is tossed aside as an option, and more than usually, left to petrify.

Arsenic and a Writer's Prerogative

In Joseph Kesselring's 1941 comedy, *Arsenic and Old Lace*, two aunts develop a nasty habit of surreptitiously bumping off elderly gentlemen with poisoned elderberry wine and burying them in their cellar, all in the name of charity for the men's aged lonesomeness. As comical as the play is, it can be a sad commentary on human nature. We so very often believe that what we are doing is the right thing, when all the while our philosophies are poison and our good intentions are laced with lies that have convinced us it's OK to completely ignore our basic beliefs.

Christians claim to want to build their lives on Truth. But in order to do that, we actually have to think—something a lot of Christians would rather not do. As the character Rachel from *Inherit the Wind* exclaims, "It seemed safer not to think at all."[3]

One thing's for sure: we won't find the truth by *not* thinking about it. If we pick up *The Da Vinci Code* and read it at face value or watch the movie and leave doubting the power and deity of our Savior, we are refusing to think. So what's the big deal? What's wrong with letting Ron Howard entertain us a little? Does anyone really give credence to a mere movie? One person voiced it this way: "The thing I don't get is . . . what is so terrifying in Dan Brown's ideas to Christian theology? Certainly none of us were alive in the time of Jesus, and so none of us can truly know. . . . Yes, there may be clues, . . . but the reality is 2,000 years in the past. It seems to me that Christians have shown an extraordinary amount of indignant righteousness over this relatively small idea. The inability to see Jesus with anything but intransigence makes it easy to give Dan Brown's ideas more credit than they are probably due."[4]

Well, as our research has shown (see chap. 3), there are just too many nonbelievers and believers alike who will take it as truth because there's no one out there shouting as loud as lovable Ron Howard and Tom Hanks to tell them otherwise. When people take *The Da Vinci Code* at face value, it becomes spiritual arsenic—a poison intended to kill. Not only that, but it also takes the esoteric mainstream; that is, it takes Brown's mystic pagan philosophy to the masses. Additionally, the novel strips Jesus of his uniqueness—especially of his deity—and it champions an anti-Christian message. Further, it promotes pagan goddess worship. Finally, this novel breeds unbelief in the traditional teaching and person of Christ. This is not something we can bury in our cellars without question or consideration.

Inherit the Wind was also fiction, but it has done real damage to the intellectual debate over what constitutes science and where the lines should be drawn between religion and education. In the final moments of *Inherit the Wind*, the character who plays the journalist covering the trial talks to the youthful academic who has been charged with teaching the youth of Tennessee about evolution. He says something quite profound, and ironic, considering the writer's point of view.

> *The name of my first long-shot was "Golden Dancer." She was in a big side window of the general store in Wakeman, Ohio. I used to stand out in the street and say to myself, "If I had Golden Dancer, I'd have everything in the world I desire." I was seven years old and a very fine judge of rocking horses. Golden Dancer had a bright red mane, blue eyes, and she was gold all over, with purple spots. When the sun hit the stirrups, she was a dazzling sight. But, she was a week's wages for my father. So Golden and I always had a plate glass window between us. But, let's see . . . it wasn't Christmas—it must have been my birthday. I woke up early that morning and there was Golden Dancer at the foot of my bed. Ma had skimped on groceries, and my father had worked nights for a month. I jumped from my bed and into the saddle and started to rock.*

*My dreams had come true. I had arrived! I had everything
that I would ever want. I rode Golden Dancer like she was a
prize race horse who was winning the Kentucky Derby. I rode
her for all she was worth—and it broke! It split in two. She
had been in the sun of the store window for so long that her
wood was rotten and her glue had dried too hard. The whole
thing was put together with spit and sealing wax! All shine; no
substance.*

Then, turning to the teacher, he says: "Bert, whenever you see
something bright, shining, and perfect-seeming—all gold with pur-
ple spots—look behind the paint. And if it's a lie—show it up for
what it really is!"[5]

How's that for irony?

Dan Brown says that faith is a continuum and that he is a
Christian—in his own way. But the views Dan Brown showcases
through his characters' discussions are irreconcilable with traditional, orthodox Christianity. We're not terrified by Dan Brown or
his ideas and we're certainly not asking you to be either. However,
ideas have consequences.

What we are saying to you, dear reader, as you look at Jesus
through the lens of any influential author, is to look behind the
paint. Grasp what is really there. Is it something authentic, something that will make you a person of consequence? Or is this bright,
shiny package merely a story that will not stand the test of time?
Don't be afraid to ask those questions. Dan Brown's pretty rocking
horse of a narrative is barely held together with spit and sealing wax.
All shine; no substance.

Whether we're fans of the thriller *The Da Vinci Code* or not, we
would all do well to follow the lead of our local Barnes and Noble
bookselling associate, Nick, who told us when we called there (and
with no prompting): "We always keep Dan Brown in fiction."

NOTES

Introduction

1. Judith Stacey, *Brave New Families* (Basic Books, 1990), 139–41.

2. Maureen O'Hara and Walter Truett Anderson, "Welcome to the Postmodern World," *Family Therapy Networker* (September/October 1991): 18–25.

Chapter 1: Why Now?

1. Michelle Orecklin, "The Novel that Ate the World," *Time* magazine, April 25, 2005.

Chapter 2: What Might Have Been

1. Judy Waggoner, "Spirituality surge felt in bookstores, radio," *Post-Crescent* (Appleton, WI), September 11, 2002.

2. The Barna Group, *Number of Unchurched Adults Has Nearly Doubled Since 1991*, May 2004.

3. Brian MacQuarrie, "Pastor Rivets Many Without Politics," *Boston Globe,* October 11, 2005.

4. Quoted in Bill Goldstein, "As a Novel Rises Quickly, Book Industry Takes Note," *New York Times*, April 21, 2003.

Chapter 3: Nailing Jell-O to a Tree

1. Daniel B. Clendenin, "Only One Way," *Christianity Today* (January 12, 1998): 35–40.
2. Roger Lundin, "The Pragmatics of Postmodernity," in *Christian Apologetics in the Postmodern World*, eds. Timothy R. Phillips and Dennis L. Ockholm (InterVarsity Press, 1995), 77.
3. Mortimer J. Adler, *Truth in Religion: The Plurality of Religions and the Unity of Truth* (Macmillan, 1990), 1–4.
4. Norman Geisler and Peter Bocchino, *Unshakable Foundations* (Bethany House, 2001), 44.
5. From *American Demographics* (January 2002).
6. George A. Lindbeck, "The Church's Mission to a Postmodern Culture," in *Postmodern Theology: Christian Faith in a Pluralist World*, ed. Frederic B. Burnham (HarperCollins, 1989), 38.
7. J. P. Moreland, *Love Your God with All Your Mind: The Role of Reason in the Life of the Soul* (NavPress, 1997).
8. Peter Kreeft, *The Snakebite Letters: Devilishly Devious Secrets for Subverting Society as Taught in Tempter's Training School* (Ignatius Press, 1998).
9. Stephen Neill, *Christian Faith and Other Faiths* (InterVarsity, 1984), 30.

Chapter 4: Quid est Veritas?

1. Geisler and Bocchino, *Unshakable Foundations*, 55.
2. Winfried Corduan, *No Doubt About It* (Broadman & Holman Publishers, 1997), 75.
3. Paul Copan, "'Who Are You to Judge Others?' In Defense of Making Moral Judgments," *Areopagus Journal* 1, no. 3 (July 2001): 30–35.
4. Anne-Geri Fann, "Waiting for God, Pt. 1," *New Wineskins* magazine, http://wineskins.blogspot.com/2005/03/waiting-for-god-pt-1.html.
5. Dr. Rosemary Clark, lecture notes on *San Manuel Bueno,*

martir, Cambridge University, http://www.mml.cam.ac.uk/spanish/
abinitio/unamuno/Unamuno-notes.html.

6. Tom Wright, *The New Testament and the People of God*
(Fortress Press, 1992), 35–36.

7. Chart adapted from Ravi Zacharias, quoting Walter Truett
Anderson, *Telling the Truth,* ed. D. A. Carson (Zondervan, 2000), 20.

8. Peter L. Berger, *The Precarious Vision* (New York:
Doubleday, 1961), 158.

9. B. F. Westcott, "The Response to the Appeal," *Borderland* 1,
no. 1 (July 1893).

Chapter 5: Don't Know Much about History

1. Gerald O'Collins, "The Da Vinci Code," *America—The
National Catholic Weekly* (December 15, 2003). See also www
.catholicweb.com.

2. For verification that this is actually happening in North
America, see Linda Burstyn's "Female Circumcision Comes to
America," *Atlantic Monthly* (October 1995): 32.

3. Alvin J. Schmidt, *How Christianity Changed the World*
(Zondervan, 2004), 122.

4. Walker Percy, *Lost in the Cosmos* (Farrar, Straus & Giroux,
1983), 201–202.

5. Reijer Hooykaas, *Religion and the Rise of Modern Science*
(Scottish Academic Press, 1972), 26.

6. Schmidt, 219–44.

7. Mortimer J. Adler, *The Great Ideas: A Lexicon of Western
Thought* (Macmillan, 1992), 307.

8. Ibid., 308.

9. Juli Cragg Hilliard, "ABC Special Examines *Da Vinci Code*
Ideas," *Publishers Weekly,* Religion Bookline.

10. Mary Lefkowitz, *Not Out of Africa: How Afrocentrism
Became an Excuse to Teach Myth as History* (HarperCollins—Basic
Books, 1996), 51, 161.

11. Ibid., 27, 35.

Chapter 6: No Double Standards Allowed?

1. Bruce Bouchner, "Does 'The Da Vinci Code' Crack Leonardo?" *New York Times,* August 3, 2003, late edition.

2. "Historians to sue over plot of 'Da Vinci Code,'" cbc.ca, October 27, 2005. See http://www.cbc.ca/story/arts/national/2005/10/27/Arts/davincisuit_051027.html.

3. L. D. Meagher, "Book Makes 'X-Files' look like 'Mr. Smith Goes to Washington,'" cnn.com reviews, February 19, 1999. See http://www.cnn.com/books/reviews/9902/19/templar.

4. William James, *The Varieties of Religious Experience,* Modern Library Paperback ed. (Random House, 1999), 552.

Chapter 7: Thanking Dan Brown

1. Intro to Salman Rushdie, "The Book Burning," *The New York Review of Books* 36, no. 3 (March 2, 1989).

2. From a letter to the *Telegraph & Argus* newspaper (Yorkshire, U.K.), quoted in "Book burning in Bradford sparks political mayhem," *Telegraph & Argus,* January 14, 1989. See http://www.this isbradford.co.uk/bradford__district/100_years/1989.html.

3. Ian Hamilton, "The First Life of Salman Rushdie," *New Yorker*, 25 December 1995–1 January 1996, 113.

4. Wikipedia, s.v. "Salman Rushdie," http://en.wikipedia.org/wiki/Salman_Rushdie#The_Satanic_Verses_controversy.

5. Dan Brown's official Web site, "Common Questions," http://www.danbrown.com/novels/davinci_code/faqs.html.

6. Rushdie, "The Book Burning."

7. Dan Brown's official Web site, "Common Questions."

8. Herbert Mitgang, "Rushdie Novel Brings Bomb Threats," *New York Times,* January 14, 1989.

9. This quote and many ideas in this section come from Paul Brians, English professor and undergraduate director at Washington State University. His study guide for *The Satanic Verses* (at http://www.wsu.edu/~brians/anglophone/satanic_verses) is invaluable.

10. *Telegraph & Argus,* "Book Burning."

11. Salman Rushdie, "Is Nothing Sacred?" (1990); http://www
.utdallas.edu/~kandula/Rushdie.pdf.

Chapter 8: Does He Have a Point?

1. Stephen Mansfield, Mansfield Group Web site's "Articles,"
"Back to the Future: the Meaning of the 1960s," http://mansfield
group.com/art_1960.html.

2. Cnn.com, "Articles," "Nixon's Press Secretary Ziegler Dies,"
11 February 2003, http://www.cnn.com/2003/ALLPOLITICS/
02/10/ziegler.obit.ap/.

3. Mansfield, "Back to the Future."

4. Marc J. Hetherington, *Why Trust Matters: Declining Political
Trust and the Demise of American Liberalism* (Princeton University
Press, 2005), 2.

5. Ibid.

6. Peter Berger, *Facing Up to Modernity: Excursions in Society,
Politics, and Religion* (Basic Books, 1977), 133.

7. Carl F. H. Henry, "Dare We Renew the Controversy?"
Christianity Today (June 24, 1957): 26.

8. D. A. Carlson, *The Gagging of God* (Zondervan, 1996),
439–40.

Chapter 10: Shooting Ourselves in the Foot?

1. Dan Burchett, *When Bad Christians Happen to Good People:
Where We Have Failed Each Other and How to Reverse the Damage*
(WaterBrook Press, 2002), 106–107.

2. Cal Thomas and Ed Dobson, *Blinded by Might: Can the
Religious Right Save America?* (Zondervan, 1999), 54.

3. Kenneth Bailey, *Poet and Peasant and Through Peasant Eyes:
A Literary-Cultural Approach to the Parables in Luke* (Eerdmans,
1976), 79.

4. Art Lindsley, *True Truth: Defending Absolute Truth in a Relativistic World* (InterVarsity Press, 2005), 50–51.

5. C. S. Lewis, *God in the Dock*, ed. Walter Hooper (Eerdmans, 1970), 93.

1. (Hen

2. *Influe*

3

4 trans

5 *Histo* –5.

6 e, see D e- *Aria*

7 6.

1 (Ban

2 n *Histo* 4/ 52.0

3

4 -
and-da-vinci-code.html.

5. Lawrence and Lee, *Inherit the Wind.*